Sorry
I DIDN'T
WRITE

NADIA ALLEYNE

To anyone told they couldn't do something;
prove them wrong!

* * *

"The only way to make sense out of change is to plunge into it,
move with it, and join the dance."

Alan Watts

TABLE OF CONTENTS

PREFACE

I suppose there is a part in all of us that is intrigued by other people's stories. By reading these stories, we hope to feel that we are not that different from everyone else. We like to be entertained. We like to identify with the struggles and successes of others. On some level, we even want someone to root for. We like to think that we have learnt something or grown in some way after reading a novel and having a shared experience with the writer.

There is something about writing about an experience you are going through and what you are learning that helps you come to terms with the experience, with your reactions to the experience and with your emotions. I worried about writing this; something about having the time to sit and think and explore those thoughts and demons seems a bit "bougie", a bit self-indulgent. I felt that every opportunity I had for a little spare time should be focused on chasing those career goals, researching how to climb further up the corporate ladder and reading books that can teach me how to "lean in" further, not taking time to be still and think and write about my experiences, reactions and emotions. The voice in my head kept saying there is just no time for reflections and writing.

But I suppose my ultimate purpose for putting pen to paper was to experience some type of catharsis. And I must say, I experienced several as I wrote this book and as I recalled aspects of my experiences and interactions in Singapore, where I am currently living, Barbados, where I grew up, and Yangon, where I spent some time. Of course, I hope (as I think most writers do) that it will help you, the reader, in some way or other. How it helps is totally up to you. If nothing else, I hope it is at least a little bit entertaining.

Love,

Nads

xoxo

ACKNOWLEDGEMENTS

Special thanks to:

My Yangon friends (you know who you are) for making my time in Yangon all that it was.

Julia, for your constant encouragement in getting this finished and published. You are the best friend a girl could ask for.

My editor, Toni Daniel,

Marguerita Goodridge and Lorna Bynoe who nurtured my love for reading and writing, and

Last but by no means least,

My husband Derek, my family and friends for putting up with me while I wrote this book.

PART ONE

SINGAPORE

Confessions of an Expat Wife

WE ARE HERE

Tuesday, March 27, 2018

*I was so tired from our flights that I don't think I formed a
first impression of the place. What I do remember thinking as
we drove to our hotel is: We are here, this will be our home
now and I am so far away from friends and family.*

We arrived at the Hotel Bencoolen on Hong Kong Street at 5:30
p.m. After a thirteen-hour flight from London, we were desperate to
set our luggage down and exhale for a moment. My husband, Derek,
who was walking slightly ahead of me, greeted the young lady at the
front desk and gave his last name. We waited in anticipation while the
young lady — Josephine — punched some keys on the keyboard for
what seemed like an eternity. Finally, she looked up and gave us the bad
news: our name wasn't in the system. There was no reservation there
for us. Apparently, there had been a mix-up with what our contact in
the Human Resources Department had communicated to my husband.
It was the first of many mix-ups we would have with that HR person.

I remember Josephine putting me to sit down in the lobby area by
reception and giving me an apple while my husband tried to contact
HR. She chatted with me about where I was from, asked about my

hair texture and recommended a salon I should visit. She told me she was studying law at university and when I told her that I am a lawyer she suggested that I teach law now that I would be living in Singapore. Despite all his efforts, my husband was having no success with messaging HR via WhatsApp. Seeing our distress, Josephine offered to liaise with HR on our behalf. She and the HR contact had what sounded like a heated exchange on the phone in a language I assumed was Mandarin and it was finally ascertained that we were supposed to be at V Hotel Bencoolen and not Hotel Bencoolen. Before we left the hotel, Josephine gave me her card and told me I should contact her if we needed anything.

It was raining by then and we went off dragging our suitcases to hail a cab. Not many people were on the street due to the downpour and, as we waited, I took in my first glimpses of Singapore and found that I was impressed by how modern the surroundings were. From my limited vantage point, I could see that Hotel Bencoolen was located in what looked to be a corporate area and was surrounded by a mix of converted shophouses and high-rise buildings with floor-to-ceiling glass panes and varying architectural designs. I don't get to see much else before a cab quickly arrives. While in the cab, my husband expressed that he felt that Josephine perhaps thought I was Indian, being Indian herself. I would eventually come to learn that she would not be the only one who mistook me for Indian here in Singapore with my tanned complexion and freshly relaxed hair that had been flat-ironed straight. It had been many years since I was mistaken for being of Indian ethnicity. When I attended law school in Trinidad and Tobago, I had, on more than one occasion, been mistaken for "dougla" and my surname "Alleyne" was, on occasion, pronounced "Ali". I suppose many people in this part of the world have no concept of Barbados or the Caribbean and didn't understand why anyone would travel over 10,000 miles from the Caribbean to come to Singapore. Therefore, she must have assumed I was from India or Sri Lanka.

We arrived at V Hotel Bencoolen after riding in the cab for about ten minutes. I was relieved that we had finally arrived so we could get some sleep. We checked in as this was where HR had booked us and we hoped that even though the reception area reminded us of a movie concession stand that things would look up once we made our way to the room. However, our fervent hopes were dashed when we finally got to our room and found that it was a lot tinier than we expected. It could barely hold our luggage. All I could do was laugh. We were, after all, relocating so we both had two suitcases each plus our carry-ons. We had just travelled eight hours from Barbados, transferred from Gatwick to Sofitel, Heathrow for a brief layover and then travelled thirteen hours from Heathrow to Singapore. My husband was livid, but all I wanted to do was shower and go to bed. So we decided that was what we would do and then try and sort out the mess in the morning. We were booked into that hotel for two weeks until we could find an apartment, but there was no way we could have a comfortable stay there for two weeks.

Wednesday, March 28, 2018

We woke up at 3 a.m. somewhat rested but famished. The hotel had no room service so we went outside in search of somewhere that would be open so we could get a bite to eat. We are usually very cautious as visitors to another country. However, we felt relatively comfortable venturing outside because we had read in our research that Singapore was a very safe place. After walking for about five minutes, we found a 7-Eleven where we got some drinks, snacks and sandwiches and went back to our room. This is when it began to sink in. We were in Singapore, approximately 10,923 miles, or 17,558 kilometres, away from Barbados. Derek seemed unbothered; he had been a serial expat in foreign countries from the time he had graduated from university in Ireland. This was just another adventure for him. He has lived in:

Austin, Texas; the San Francisco Bay Area; Bucharest; Budapest; Richmond, Surrey; Italy for eleven years; Paris; Jamaica; St. Lucia and Barbados. In fact, we met when he was living in St. Lucia and had visited Barbados for a workshop. Besides Trinidad for law school from 2006 to 2008, Myanmar on secondment in 2014 and one year in St. Lucia between 2016 and 2017, this would be my first time living anywhere outside of Barbados.

We were severely jet lagged and could not sleep as our internal clocks had not yet adjusted and it was only three in the afternoon in Barbados. With nothing left to do, we began to earnestly research hotels online as there was no way we would be staying at our current one for another day, far less two weeks. We settled on Novotel Clarke Quay since the reviews online were good and it seemed to be in the thick of things, with various restaurants and nightclubs in a historic riverside area called Clarke Quay. The quay is located upstream from the Singapore River which was very important in the colonial days. All we had to do was wait until morning to get HR to sort things out. We eventually fell back to sleep.

Our first full day in Singapore was spent staying on top of HR to get our move sorted, walking around our environs, deciding on where to eat, getting our bearings and then finally moving to Novotel Clarke Quay sometime in the evening. Novotel Clarke Quay and V Hotel Bencoolen were like chalk and cheese. The staff at Novotel were very professional and welcoming. Also, the hotel was clean and modern with red furniture and mirrors lining the walls, and we could tell it was bustling with activity as evidenced by the line of guests coming and going. Since we were staying so long, we were escorted along a red carpet to the elevator where we got the executive check-in on the 24th floor in the premier lounge. With the executive check-in for "long stay" guests we would have access to the premier lounge that served a nice breakfast buffet and varied, tasty appetisers and drinks in the evening. There were also amazing views of Clarke Quay and we could see the famous Marina Bay Sands (an architectural wonder to behold) and the Singapore Flyer (think London Eye) in the distance. Things were beginning to look up.

I notified the real estate agent who was supposed to show us around the following day that we had changed hotels and confirmed the time that she would pick us up in the morning to show us apartments. We were booked in the hotel for a maximum of two weeks and we had a limited time before Derek started his new role, so we wanted to find somewhere quickly so that he wouldn't have to take time off to view apartments once he started work.

Thursday, March 29, 2018

Elizabeth, our real estate agent, arrived promptly at 10 a.m. like she said she would. From the start she was a godsend. I found her online one day while researching places and areas to live from Barbados. She was affiliated with a top real estate company that I was familiar with in Barbados so I knew what the company was capable of. Plus, she was a female. I felt that Derek would feel more comfortable if I was dealing with a female, in the event that he had to leave me to view places on my own while he was at work, if it had to come down to that. I had reached out to her on the internet and our appointments for viewing a few places were arranged. After a few days of checking out apartments, we settled on a newish condo near the Central Business District. We signed a two-year lease and made the transition from our hotel to our new condo. Our life in Singapore had begun.

UNEXPECTED WEIGHT GAIN

Friday, April 13, 2018

For years I had tried to gain weight and was unable to put on any. I would eat every and anything and still not gain an ounce. I ate so much at family events sometimes that my cousins would refer to me as "slim pig".

Up until the time I got married in December 2016 I had weighed 95 pounds. When we moved back to Barbados in September 2017 from St. Lucia, I was still only about 100 pounds. In the Caribbean, women with thick legs, large backsides and "meat on their bones" are valued above other body types. I even remember once my doctor telling me during one of my appointments that I needed to put on weight. Not too much, he had said, just "a five pound" or so. Interestingly enough, this was not because he was concerned that my current weight posed a health challenge. Instead, he simply thought that if I wanted to find a man I needed to gain some weight. He had been the family's doctor for years and we had developed a rapport over time, so his comments were just part of the banter we both engaged in whenever I visited his office. He even offered to prescribe a tonic so I could eat more and grow a bumper like Barbados' Soca Queen Alison Hinds.

Fast forward to Singapore. We arrived in Singapore at the end of March and in just a few weeks my weight had soared. My husband is a "fatist" which, according to the Urban Dictionary, is a person who has a deep dislike or even mistrust of the overweight. With regards to the opposite sex, a "fatist" could be considered antithetical to a "chubby chaser". In Singapore, we were surrounded by skinny ladies. I was told that in Asian cultures the skinnier you are, the more successful you are perceived to be, which is a sharp contrast to some African cultures where the fatter you are the wealthier you are perceived to be, or in the Caribbean where, when you gain weight, everyone takes it as a sign that you are living well.

When I lived in Barbados, I did yoga and I ran. Back then, neither activity was pursued with any consistency, but then I wasn't struggling to lose weight. I had never understood before the struggles involved with dieting until I got here and my weight seemed to be steadily increasing. In the Caribbean, I had a fairly regimented eating schedule with all meals more or less at the same time each day. In Singapore, the loss of home, familiar surroundings and friends caused me to comfort eat at all hours of the day and make less than healthy eating choices. Food is readily available at the restaurants located downstairs our condo, so on any given day you can eat from Japanese to French to Thai to Peruvian to Italian. If you get bored of those restaurants, there are a plethora of other restaurants across the street in Haji Lane with its colourful shophouses, or one street over to Arab Street where you can get your Mediterranean, Persian, Turkish or Lebanese cuisine. If none of these satisfy your tastebuds, you can go to the mall which is not too far away with standalone restaurants, or the food court where you can choose from local food to fast food. The set lunch menus (three course meals for an affordable price) did not help matters. I tend not to be a dessert person, but if it is included in the set lunch price I might as well have it.

In a panic, I looked up exercise regimes on Google and researched how the likes of Victoria Beckham and Halle Berry stayed fit and youthful. The final straw that broke the camel's back, however, happened after I posted a picture on Instagram. Someone commented that I seemed determined to eat my way through Singapore. That did it. I promptly deleted that picture and I took a long look in the mirror and realised this development could not continue. I resolved to make healthier eating choices and I stopped overeating. Derek and I stopped eating heavy dinners in the evening and we ran/walked for five kilometres three mornings a week at 5:45 a.m. I could not believe it! After years of trying to gain weight without success, my body finally decided to cooperate at the head time I most certainly was not trying to gain weight. Talk about betrayal!

IT WAS THE BEST OF TIMES

Saturday, April 13, 2019

I knew at some point that my husband Derek had been interviewed for the role of Chief Operations Officer for Singapore and Malaysia at a company in South East Asia. However, for some reason, I had failed to process it in my mind that we were actually going to have to relocate if he got the role.

The position would see him based in Singapore. When he told me that he got the position it was like when someone speaks to you and you see their lips moving and still you are not really hearing what they are saying. Perhaps I had refused to process it since I had only just moved back to Barbados after living in St. Lucia for a year and was happy to be back on my 166 square miles. St. Lucia wasn't that far away from Barbados, so any time we were feeling claustrophobic or I just had to have some pudding and souse or my Auntie Ann's fishcakes we could escape to Barbados for the odd weekend here and there. I knew there would be none of that when we moved to Singapore. As I sit back now and recall how things unfolded, everything happened very quickly. He went through the interview rounds, got an offer and we had a few weeks to pack, say our goodbyes and dine at our favourite places for one last time.

It has been one year since we have been living here in Singapore. They say that time flies when you are having fun and I feel as though our first year here sped by. Derek got a promotion at work to Chief Executive Officer and we are both delighted that his hard work and long hours at the office paid off. In terms of the actual city, we are impressed by how modern the surroundings are. Gardens by the Bay is an architectural wonder to behold. It reminds me of something you would see in a futuristic sci-fi movie. The solar-powered fifty-metre-high super trees at Gardens by the Bay take my breath away. Each super tree has tropical flowers and various ferns running over its steel framework. Visitors to the gardens can walk across bridges called skywalks which connect several of the giant super trees — a definite "don't" if you have vertigo or are afraid of heights.

Even though the country is small (about 278 square miles), it doesn't feel crammed. Everything is fairly spread out and I am surprised by the number of green spaces available for a city and how remarkably clean it is. One of the measures the country has put in place to keep the city spotless is the banning of chewing gum. The population is majority ethnic Chinese and this is evident in the food, which can range from Cantonese to Hainanese (where Singapore gets its national dish chicken rice), Hakka, Teochew and Hokkien. The remainder of the population, which is about 25%, is made up of Malays, Indians and expats. We like how calm and orderly everything is and we are pleased that the MRT (Mass Rapid Transit) is clean and runs on time.

I have started going to church at the St. Andrew's Cathedral on Thursday afternoons at 12:30 for weekday prayers. St. Andrew's Cathedral is one MRT stop away from where I live which is probably a three minute ride. I could walk it (approximately 1.2 km), but the weather is too hot and humid for that. I prefer to go at this time as the church is less crowded with only about thirty or so of us in total (sometimes less) scattered in the pews. At this hour, it is mostly older people, a few executives still wearing their access cards on lanyards around their necks, housewives and tourists.

I have not written for some time. I had been completing my LLM in International Commercial Law over the last year, so I had been doing writing of a different type. I got back my results and it turns out I got a merit. Initially I had not planned on doing an LLM, but after careful consideration, I felt this was a good opportunity to upskill, learn some new things and challenge myself. I loved the entire journey — meeting new people, the actual modules as well as researching and writing my dissertation. This is in direct contrast to when I did my LLB and attended law school. Being older and more mature now, I adopted a more disciplined mindset in the way I approached my masters studies. I am pleased with my merit.

I felt like writing this evening since we went to the yacht show — partly to celebrate my merit and mostly because we love boats — and I felt I had to chronicle it. The Singapore Yacht Show on Sentosa Island is really phenomenal. It is a four-day event of super yachts, glamorous day-to-night parties, lots of champagne and some of the sleekest Lamborghinis and Ferraris. The show is fabulously organised, from collecting your entry wrist bands to the booths displaying every manner of yacht you could think of to the food and beverage options on the marina. There is truly something for everyone wanting to own or rent a boat, yacht or superyacht — or those interested in the yachting lifestyle. Derek and I really enjoy being around and on boats. We got our sailing licences when we lived in St. Lucia. Derek is a bareboat skipper and I am a flotilla skipper so the yacht show is of particular interest to us as we have dreams of owning our own vessel one day.

This was our second year attending the show. That there is even a show of this type means that yachts must be selling, yet it is hard to believe that there are people in the world who actually own these types of vessels. This year we did the VIP experience which was excellent. See why I was so excited to write? Derek even met the lady whose husband started the show. It was a huge contrast to the first year when, hot and sticky, we gave up looking at the boats relatively early and went in search of drink and food. That year we had only just arrived in Singapore and saw an advertisement for the show by chance. What we did this year was book a room at the W on Sentosa — a luxurious island resort ideally positioned beside the marina where the yacht show is held — had lunch at the hotel's restaurant and then changed our attire for the yacht show and got a lift on the hotel's caddy car over to the show. All the while "Big Pimpin'" by Jay Z is playing in my head. I had to resist the urge to sing it out loud, lest the caddy car driver look at me funny. We walked around the air-conditioned booths and spent our time in the VIP lounge drinking champagne, eating canapés and watching smartly dressed, beautiful people of every ethnicity that makes up Singapore's melting pot. When evening rolled around and the sun was less menacing we went to explore the yachts by Princess, Ferretti and others. The various sponsorship banners were fluttering in the wind and the atmosphere was lively, fun-filled and social. The Ferretti Yachts seemed to be the most popular and everyone wanted to take pictures by them. When we had our fill, we went back to our room overlooking the marina to take in the rest of the vibes from the comfort of our balcony. As I recount the experience, I have to say it was one of the best I have had in Singapore so far and I am utterly grateful. Life can be filled with such challenges at times that it is always a good thing when you can have some good experiences interspersed with all the rubbish.

WHEN SU COMES TO VISIT

Wednesday, April 17, 2019

We have been living here for one year now and guess how many visitors we've had? One would think that since we jetted off to a far-flung location that we would have a long queue of friends and family eagerly waiting to take the opportunity to visit us in an exotic location. But that has not been the case. We have had zero visitors, until my friend Su messaged me a few weeks ago to tell me that she had booked a flight for her, her partner Eric and the kids to visit.

When I was leaving Myanmar in 2014 both Su and I were sad. We had been colleagues during my secondment in Yangon, Myanmar in 2014 and she had embraced me like a sister. We had become really close and we vowed that we would see each other again. We didn't know when and we didn't know how, but we vowed it would happen. I had always imagined that she would come visit me in Barbados and bring the girls and we would spend glorious days at the beach. But five years later we were meeting up in Singapore. It is true what they say — you never know where life will take you or how life will pan out. Neither of us thought at the time that I would now be living in Singapore, a mere three-hour flight from Yangon, Myanmar. The girls are now 12 and 9 years old, all grown up and no longer babies. They were just two mischievous little things when I first met them at 6 and 3 years old.

It is Water Festival time in Myanmar which marks the New Year there. The festival is celebrated over five days, which means time off from work and school. Su took the opportunity to plan a holiday in Singapore with the girls and Eric. To say that I am excited to see Su and the girls again after five years is an understatement. We stayed in touch since I left Myanmar and we are still great friends. I am also excited for her to finally meet Derek. Su knew all about Derek, when Derek and I met and when we eventually got married, but she has never actually met him in person. We agreed to meet up for dinner this evening at Wine Connection at Robertson Walk which is a few days after they arrived.

When Su and I are finally reunited, we spend several minutes hugging and chatting excitedly before we actually settle down. I can't get over how much the girls have grown and I am grateful that they love their Easter gifts which Derek and I foraged the mall for once we knew they were coming and it would be Easter time. Su and I sit next to each other so that she can fill me in on everything in her life and Yangon. We leave the men to chat about whatever men chat about while the girls play with their mobile phones. She tells me that I would probably not recognise Yangon now. Some of the spots that we frequented are no more; Union Bar and The Lab have both closed down and new places have sprung up. The company we were both working for when we met was acquired by another company and she has a new role in procurement and loves it. She had been getting a bit restless in her government relations role and wanted a new challenge. We ordered food and copious amounts of wine while the girls take pictures of us with funny filters. We are happy to be in each other's company once more, even if it is only for a short time. Despite the years that have passed, we are still firm friends.

FINDING A JOB

Saturday, April 20, 2019

A few weeks before Derek and I were to move to Singapore we were sitting at the Rum Shack at Royal Westmoreland, a luxury and golfing resort located on the west coast of Barbados, when we met Marianne. We were living at Royal Westmoreland at the time and would go to Rum Shack after particularly stressful days to relax and unwind. Rum Shack was themed after traditional rum shops seen around the island serving spirits, fishcakes, traditional flying fish cutters, Caribbean rotis and grilled pork chops among other delicious dishes.

The atmosphere there was a bit more relaxed and casual than the clubhouse where we would sometimes eat Sunday lunch. Marianne's daughter took tennis lessons at the tennis courts which are next to the Rum Shack restaurant at the resort and Marianne would normally drive in her Jaguar and drop her off. However, one evening as she was walking to the tennis courts with her daughter, she and Derek happened to strike up a conversation about her Jaguar. She took up Derek's invitation to join us and the rest, as they say, is history. It wasn't long before the conversation moved from cars, to our respective professions. Marianne's husband was the owner of a successful business on the island and she spent her time helping him with the business and looked after their daughter. Marianne, after learning that I would soon become a housewife when we relocated to Singapore, felt that I should embrace it and have a child or two, but I couldn't take Marianne's advice seriously as being a housewife was never something I had envisioned for myself.

I suppose that many people would be happy to be where I am, and I actually feel guilty at times that I am somehow being ungrateful. I feel like everything is on hold or on pause and still the days are rushing ahead. While I respect women who choose to work exclusively inside the home and devote their time and energy to managing the household, raising children and looking after their husbands, I just never thought it was for me. From the time I was about seven, I had it drilled in my head how important it is for a woman to be independent, to have and make her own money and chart her own path. Perhaps, as I got older, I had seen enough Lifetime movies where somehow the housewife always ended up getting the short end of the stick in these situations. That was never a position that I wanted to find myself in. However, I did think this was the perfect time to do a master's degree and buy myself some time away from work but give the appearance that I was still doing something productive.

Once I completed my master's, I hadn't thought that finding another job would be difficult — I have educational and professional qualifications coupled with life experience. Yet, finding a job in Singapore eludes me and I find myself slipping more and more into the role of housewife. I just can't reconcile in my mind what others expect of me (to be working and climbing the career ladder), what I expect of myself (to be working and excelling at a role and climbing the career ladder), and what I have essentially become (a housewife). My typical day involves planning what we would eat for dinner, whether it was something I would make or if we would go out. Depending on the day, it may include going to church in the afternoon, grocery shopping, taking my husband's shirts to the dry cleaners or running some other errand for him to make his life easier. Fridays are reserved for cleaning the apartment — the first time in my life that this task isn't outsourced. If Derek has to travel to Malaysia or Bangkok for business meetings, I accompany him and explore the place while he works. I have gone from advising the C-suite and sitting on the senior management team at my company in Barbados to being a housewife. I am miserable, but I have to try hard not to make Derek miserable when he finally gets home from work. I miss the feeling of being productive and the routine of going to work. Somehow, we often link our jobs to identity, and I am struggling to cope with the sudden loss of identity and purpose.

It doesn't help that you can't do much here without your husband. His right to work in Singapore is legitimised with an employment pass which his company sponsors while my right to be in Singapore is legitimised by a dependant pass, and the government-issued identification card clearly states "Dependent Pass". I can only work in Singapore if I get a letter of consent from the Ministry of Manpower or if whichever company decides to hire me applies for an employment pass. I cannot set up a mobile phone account without him and if I need to change my SIM card for my mobile, I need to produce a letter signed by him just to get a new SIM card. It is frustrating.

Sunday, April 21, 2019

I get so scared about the future sometimes. I have applied for a few legal roles. I even shelled out to have my CV professionally done. Perhaps I should have done this a year ago while I was doing my master's, but you know what they say — better late than never. I think the longer I am without a job, the more depressed I am becoming. I go to check the mailbox and it seems very funny that there is an application for part-time positions as postal workers. It is as if the universe is laughing at me.

I just want to sleep all day today. If I tell Derek that the reason I want to stay in bed is because I am feeling depressed, he will simply say that I have nothing to be depressed about. "Lots of people would like to be in your position" says the husband whose career is soaring while mine is languishing. Seriously! Telling someone people have it worse is a really terrible way to help someone feel better.

As I lie in bed, still in my pyjamas at noon and contemplating my life choices, I remember that a week ago I had signed up to help with a charity that provides free horse therapy to disabled children and adults. I used to go riding in the parish of St. Andrew in my native Barbados when I was younger. As I understand it, all I would have to do is walk alongside the disabled person while they ride and give them a sense of comfort. One volunteer leads the horse and the other two flank the rider on either side. That couldn't be too difficult, I thought, and it may make me feel better too, so it may be as much for them as it is for me. I also emailed the National Library about their reading-to-kids programme, but they haven't responded to me yet either. These places must have a ton of volunteers so there is probably no rush to get back to one lowly person.

GOING TO THE GYM

Wednesday, June 12, 2019

The months are rolling by and I still haven't found a job. I do have to say, though, that I got a screening call with Facebook and a recruiter rang me about a position at a telecoms company here. For these I am grateful. At least I know there isn't a problem with my CV, as it has got me noticed.

As I walk to the Salad Stop downstairs to collect my lunch, I say a little prayer: "Lord, I thank you for the break from the corporate world. Thank you very much. I am ready to go back now." Something about it being rainy today gives me comfort. It is a reminder that through every storm, God is there. He is in the midst of things. I had downloaded some free books on my Kindle and two were devotionals. I have set out on a mission to become healthier, which also includes watching what I put inside my body. I go to the gym at the same time every day, mostly around 10:00 a.m., in the hopes that I can have the gym for myself. Save for an Asian lady, I mostly get it to myself so that I can work out in peace. She doesn't bother me too much as she uses the elliptical which is on the other side of the gym and I run on the treadmill. I usually hate it if there is someone else on the treadmill next to me. It always seems as though that person is secretly judging you or competing against you, so I prefer to be alone to compete against myself and listen to my Best of Sean Paul playlist in peace. I used to say to myself that I would never be one of those housewives who goes to the gym every day. Having now found myself in that same exact situation, I can truly say that I understand why they do it. Apart from it taking some of the monotony out of the day, there is this constant fear that your husband will find a more attractive, younger (and, in my case, Asian) version, so I understand the additional motivation to go to the gym almost daily. I have to admit that I am beginning to feel and look more like myself.

YOUR GIFT WILL
MAKE ROOM FOR YOU

Thursday, June 13, 2019

Bit by bit I am coming out of the funk I have been in and seeing things from a different perspective. Today I received a poignant piece of advice via a video someone posted on LinkedIn. God knows entirely best and I don't know why I ever doubted Him.

The video, titled "How to Stay Motivated After Getting Laid Off", was recorded during a segment of *Steve Harvey* (the talk show) where he was responding to a question from a male guest in the audience. While I wasn't laid off, I can relate to what the guy was going through since I am going through the job-hunting process myself. In the video, the guest asks Steve for advice on how to stay motivated when job hunting. He goes on to explain that the job-hunting process is frustrating since for every job he applies he is being told he is either over-qualified or under-qualified for the role.

In the three-minute video, Steve completely changes the guest's perspective — and mine! He encourages him to see being laid off from his sales rep job at a computer store as an opportunity to finally pursue his true passion for and gift in the culinary arts. Steve Harvey tells the guy that he doesn't need to stay motivated; he has been given a second chance to move on to do exactly what he is supposed to be doing. God is *slick*, Steve explains, and has caused him to experience this lay-off because He is pushing him to where he needs to be. He should be using his gift and not going against what it is he was created for.

Steve advises him to grab hold of the opportunity, get a position as a cook, go to culinary school and do what he is supposed to be doing. The gentleman says he has considered doing just that, but he has been paralysed by the fear of failing. Steve stops him in his tracks and shares his experience of losing everything he ever owned and how that was a stepping stone to the success he now enjoys, doing what he loves. Just before the video ends, Steve quotes a Bible verse from Proverbs 18 that stuck with me. He said, "Your gift will make room for you and put you in the presence of great men."

This was exactly what I needed to hear today. It caused me to reflect on my own situation and realise that the delay in finding a job could be my blessing in disguise. I resolve that I will appreciate this time at home more and not be so restless to get back into the corporate world. The pace I had previously been going at was not sustainable anyway and could have led to serious burnout, so perhaps this was God's way of giving me exactly what He knew I needed.

LAZY DAYS AND POLITICS

Saturday, June 15, 2019

I suppose that I must accept that there will always be some days that are more productive than others - for writing, for my new exercise regime and for my healthy diet. I simply did not wish to go to the gym today. I was feeling very tired and decided it was probably best to rest. My resolve to stay inside today and laze around has afforded me the opportunity to catch up with politics.

Since I have been in Singapore, I have taken up staying abreast of politics in Asia which has provided more nail-biting action and intrigue than the steamiest of thrillers. As I watch the news, Hong Kong's Chief Executive, Carrie Lam, is clinging to power after being forced to suppress a controversial extradition bill due to massive protests in the street. Despite her suspension of the bill, protesters still demanded her resignation, among other requests. Clashes between protesters and the police escalated, causing Lam to face criticism over what many saw as the destruction of human rights in Hong Kong. That another female, Theresa May, was recently forced to resign as Prime Minister of the UK does not escape my thoughts and I cannot help but draw a comparison.

Hillary Clinton also crosses my mind. They are all very capable women in their own right, yet are constantly being undermined. I cannot help but wonder if these women were set up to fail. Thankfully Barbados' own Prime Minister, the Right Honourable Mia Mottley, and New Zealand's Jacinda Ardern are proving to be formidable leaders. Jacinda's leadership in the wake of the gruesome Christ Church terrorist attack was an inspiration to us all, and Ms. Mottley's approach to Barbados' debt reduction is commendable. This gives me a measure of hope that, one day, having effective female leaders will be the norm rather than the exception.

MAKING FRIENDS
AS AN ADULT

Thursday, October 3, 2019

Last night we attended the opening of a new restaurant located downstairs our building. Derek makes friends easily, so we got a special invite by the owner, Mandy, who is Chinese Malaysian but has been living in Singapore for a long time. The food and drinks were complimentary from 6 p.m. to 8 p.m.

People seem to be drawn to Derek. He does have a sense of humour and I suppose that his white skin doesn't hurt either. Mandy and her husband planned the event to coincide with Mandy's birthday and we were thrilled to be a part of the dual celebration. It was a lovely evening and we enjoyed ourselves. It was a chance to get dressed up, sample the menu that the restaurant would be offering and experience a bit of Chinese culture. As is customary for auspicious occasions, like the Chinese New Year or the opening of a new business, there was a lion dance at this restaurant's opening to chase away evil spirits and welcome in prosperous times. Traditionally, this dance requires two persons — one to manipulate the *papier-mâché* head of the lion and another to act as its hind legs. The two dancers are joined by a colourful cloth of yellows and reds which makes up the lion costume. The lion performs a series of acrobatic stances to the troupe of musicians playing gongs and cymbals and drums as evil dislikes loud noises. Someone dressed as the Chinese god of fortune blessed the business with success. It was an entertaining spectacle and I even got the opportunity to bang the gong which was at the entrance to the restaurant.

We ended up sharing a table with two other couples and a lady whose husband is based overseas — all the owner's friends whom she met while she was an expat in the Philippines. Besides Mandy who is running the restaurant and another lady, Rose, who does marketing for Changi Airport, the other ladies appear to just be involved in raising their families. Rose, whose husband is overseas, did confess that she is a private hire driver, but she just does that as a kind of side hustle in addition to ferrying her children around to their various activities. She is Singaporean and the reason she is back in Singapore is because her son, who is 17, will soon be going off to college in the UK, so she wants him to get familiar with fending for himself and being more independent. In the Philippines, she explained, they had drivers and security so it would have been hard for him to be independent there.

As I sat there listening, I couldn't help but think about how difficult it is to make friends as an adult. The conversation was mainly about when they were expats in the Philippines or about their children and I have never been to the Philippines nor do I have any children. The only time I was able to join in the conversation was when it turned to a discussion about the Korean drama *Sky Castle* (a satirical drama series about upper-class parents in South Korea which I happened to binge-watch one day out of sheer boredom).

As a child, in our teens, or even in our 20s, we generally tend not to have too many expectations from our friendships, and at these early stages in our lives we don't tend to create friendships with any prior preferences in mind. We are also not jaded yet or so suspicious of new people. However, as we get older and our time to invest in relationships gets more limited, we tend to be more cautious with whom we choose to spend our time and who we let into our lives. There is no adulting guidebook on how to actually make friends or how to find out whether others are even interested in expanding their social circle. Perhaps I have simply opted out even before I have started.

I used to be one of those persons who secretly judged expat women while being envious of their seemingly perfect lives and expat packages. After all, they get to travel to far-flung exotic locations and hang out with other expat women all day drinking white wine or gin and tonic. Now that I am an expat wife myself and have actually spoken to a few expat wives, I can tell you our lives are not perfect. We are there at the mercy of our husbands and our husbands' companies. We have to eke out lives and existences for ourselves. I used to think all expats were the same but, as with any group, there is also a class structure of sorts among expats. There are the ones who are on all-expenses-paid packages, the ones on partially paid packages and then those who are footing the bill for everything themselves. In many instances, we do not choose this life and, in most cases, we have no choice but to follow our husbands.

When you live in a foreign country, you lose that sense of community. It takes ages to build up decent friendships and, while some people tend to be welcoming, there is always that guarded, suspicious air hovering over matters — what some may refer to as "side looking with a jaundiced eye". Somehow, along the way, someone portrayed expat life as glamorous and something to be sought after, but I can assure you it is not at all glamorous.

VICTORY AT LAST?

Wednesday, April 29, 2020

Oh, I forgot to mention that I got the job I had been praying for, which is part of the reason I haven't written in a very long time. The months seem to just be flying by. I prayed about it and I went to church and adopted a different mindset and mentality in relation to my job search. I made peace with the fact that I will get the right role and the role that God intended for me in the company and legal team He wants me to be in at the right time.

It all happened so quickly that I didn't have time to write. It was a secondment position as a legal consultant with a Telco here. I was asked to interview with the company on the 13th of February, having returned from Bangkok on the weekend of February 8 just before the Government started issuing stay-at-home notices for travellers because of the COVID-19 pandemic. Derek had a leadership meeting in Bangkok and, as was the norm, instead of staying in Singapore I accompanied him. I was told I got the gig on February 14 and started on Monday, February 17. I was over the moon. Since I have previous

Telco experience, they thought I would be a great fit. I don't even know where to start to tell you all that has happened so I will just start.

It is good to get the experience of working in Singapore, and, by extension, exposure to matters in New Zealand and Australia. I don't love it, though, but I am grateful. The actual tasks are generally fine and not too difficult due to my previous Telco background. It was the commute and dealing with people that posed a challenge for me. The commute to the office was arduous. It started with three stops from home on the MRT line, then two flights of escalators, a switch to the North South Line for three more stops and finally a ten-minute walk to the office. Then I repeated the reverse on evenings. On the mornings that I just couldn't bear the thought of taking the MRT, I would use my Grab app (South East Asia's equivalent of Uber), but then I ran the risk of sometimes getting caught in traffic. As it relates to my colleagues, some people are okay, but others really make you wonder why you got out of your bed in the morning. Some people like to pretend they are so busy that they don't have time to answer a question like a civilised human being. No one has a monopoly on being busy. We are all busy and I am not sure if some people acted like they were extremely busy so that no one would approach them and ask them a question.

I am grateful, though, that I am able to assist my family in Barbados from the money I earned. That helps me to get through some days. Since I undertook this secondment, the world has been plagued by the pandemic known as COVID-19 which has necessitated me working from home. COVID-19 is an infectious disease caused by the newly discovered variant of the coronavirus and which spreads primarily through droplets of saliva or discharge from the nose when an infected person coughs or sneezes.

I know this COVID-19 period has been difficult for many around the world. Families have been forced to be isolated in their homes for extended periods, economies have been destabilised and, up to this point, there have been over one million deaths worldwide due to this novel coronavirus. Singapore's swift response to the pandemic resulted in the country having one of the lowest mortality rates for COVID-19 worldwide and I am grateful for this. Also, working from home cut out the commute and has helped me maintain my physical distance from some people with negative energy that can be draining. I am grateful that Derek and I have been able to spend more time together since we both have been working from home. We are able to schedule our lunch and coffee breaks together. We get a better understanding of each other and the work stresses we encounter each day as we are seeing it first-hand and sometimes overhearing the video calls. It has been enjoyable. I think we both needed this time together. We have established a sort of routine every day which is actually nice. Derek set up himself in the dining room and I have taken over the living room. I would take a video call any day over having to go into the office. The more grateful you are, the more things you find to be grateful for.

LIFE IN THE TIME
OF COVID-19

Thursday, May 14, 2020

As I mentioned earlier, the Singapore Government's response to the pandemic has been swift and decisive, but they had previous experience dealing with SARS (Severe Acute Respiratory Syndrome) in 2003 and MERS (Middle East Respiratory Syndrome) in 2015. Since April, the Government implemented what is known as the "circuit breaker" to contain the COVID-19 pandemic.

The measures included the closure of all non-essential workplaces where businesses were encouraged to implement work-from-home arrangements, closure of all schools, preschools, education, enrichment and student care centres (except for essential care), closure and suspension of religious activities and restrictions on movement and gatherings. Food establishments were only allowed to offer takeaway, drive-thru and delivery services. One of the earliest measures to be implemented was the mandatory wearing of masks on April 14. If you are caught not wearing a mask outside your home, you can be fined.

With all these restrictions, life has certainly changed. Take, for example, the telemedicine appointment I had a few days ago. I dread going to the doctor here in Singapore. After two years we still haven't found a great doctor that we both like. There are plenty of good, qualified doctors out there, but we just haven't found one that we can connect with. I found one the other day because I needed to fill a prescription. Certain medication that you can buy with ease over the counter in Barbados requires a prescription here. I had the appointment via telemedicine because this is the preferred method of seeing patients now due to the pandemic. This doctor also operates a clinic for COVID-19 patients who visit in the afternoon, so she books her appointments with her other patients so that they are not in the office at the same time as her COVID-19 patients. I really like her; however, she is not covered by our insurance, so I won't be able to continue seeing her. Talk about a bummer. Now is not the time to be sick. Not that there is ever a time to be sick.

Even before the pandemic, we always got most of our groceries delivered, especially the essentials like water and toilet paper, pasta, canned soups, rice — anything in a package or can except for our fruits, vegetables and bread; I liked picking those out myself. But now I have no choice but to leave it up to the supermarket staff and hope for the best. Because of the increased demand as more people are having their groceries delivered, a cap has been placed on the number of items that can be ordered to prevent hoarding and we have had to wake up early so we could get the limited available delivery slots. We went for days without seeing anyone except for delivery persons.

Luckily, I got in a hairdresser appointment before the stricter measures were implemented or my hair would have been a right mess. I think the thing which got to me most during this period was that, due to the restrictions on travel and the number of people who can gather in one place, when a close family friend died (not from COVID-19) we were unable to attend the funeral in person and could only tune in online. That made a sad situation even worse and caused me to take the death harder than I may have under normal circumstances.

Today's devotional reading was a reminder that I have trusted God before and I can do it again. These reminders are good. They bring a sense of hope and calm to me as I navigate this new normal. I take comfort in the fact that nothing comes to you that has not passed through God's providential fingers first and I try to rest in that.

FAITH IS A MUST

Tuesday, May 26, 2020

May I never forget that God has done it before and He will certainly do it again. That was the gist of this morning's devotional reading.

I have been trying to be more consistent with these readings and, in doing so, I have realised that they have been important in helping me to bring a level of calm to the start of my day. I can start my days less anxious having read a word from my devotions. I must confess, I woke up a little anxious this morning, but after reading the devotional for today I felt much better. The reading today asked that we take time to remember a specific instance in which God provided for us and celebrate it. The premise of this action is that it will increase our ability to trust Him.

It helped me to reflect, as well, on the fact that I was so worried about my stalled career, but in God's perfect timing I got the role I wanted. All my panicking was for nothing. That was my specific instance. There have been many other instances in my life when God has been there, when it was only by His divine intervention that I got through the circumstance. I am not sure if I would have made it through some challenges to where

I am today if I didn't have faith. Faith gives you that inner resolve to push through. And push through I did, growing up in less than ideal circumstances in beautiful Barbados.

PART TWO

BARBADOS
166 Square Miles

IT TAKES A VILLAGE

For all its imperfections, I love the 166 square miles that is Barbados. The reality is that nowhere is perfect, but I feel fortunate to have grown up there, in that part of the world, in the time that I did. Barbadians are a proud and resilient people. Too often we refuse to acknowledge our early years and how they affect other periods in our lives and the decisions that we ultimately make. I know these years shaped me and have given some insight into who I am.

My mother was never the most affectionate person. She was not the hugs and kisses type. Instead, she showed her love by working hard, cooking, cleaning and providing. She was a single mother trying to raise a child the best way she knew how. Like many Barbadian parents, she ensured I had a solid Christian upbringing which meant Sunday School every Sunday followed by the church service and then back to church in the evening for youth group. I remember returning home one Sunday after Sunday School, not wanting to attend the church service that came after, and being promptly sent back. My Sundays were all churched out. If, for whatever reason my mother was not attending church herself, she would send me with one of her friends. I had to ensure I completed any homework on Friday evening or Saturday because not even incomplete homework was a reason for me being allowed to stay home from church. Illness was the only acceptable reason for absence from church and, even then, it would have had to be a serious illness that required a medical doctor prescribing bed rest or time at home as part of the treatment. If the church had a week of revival services you better believe I had to go. I had so much church in me I eventually became a Sunday School teacher and held various roles in the youth group from secretary to treasurer to vice president and eventually president.

Another thing that was a non-negotiable for my mother was education. An education would get you noticed and hired which would be your vehicle to being independent and improving your life. I remember when I was 8 years old, I was involved in a Christmas gift exchange at our church. The lady who drew my name asked me what I would like as a gift. I was excited and thought about all the possibilities: Nancy Drew books, a doctor play set, a Monopoly game, Snakes and Ladders, a puzzle. My mother, however, told me to ask for school shoes. I was a little disappointed, but I wasn't surprised that my mother wanted me to ask for something school-related. That was how much she focused on education and wanted me to do the same, even at Christmas.

It is true what they say — it really takes a village to raise a child. Somebody will give you a breadfruit, some mangoes, a hand of bananas or a bag of limes to make lemonade for days. Your uncle with the farm will send down some things. You will never go hungry. I recall family, neighbours and members of the congregation always bringing us items and, likewise, when our mango tree or lime tree or soursop tree was bearing, we would share the produce with others. Barbados is a wonderful place if you have the means to enjoy it, and if you don't, you can always count on your family, your neighbours and your church to help. When someone helps you and they are also struggling, that's not mere assistance, that is love. Barbadians have a way of rallying around each other.

Growing up, my mother had the support of my grandparents, my great grandparents, my aunts and uncle who all lived nearby and I got to grow up with my cousin Toni who is close to my age. If we weren't family, though, I don't know that our paths would have ever crossed. We are like chalk and cheese, to say the least. She was not one to focus on school and maybe even downright disliked it. Persons are always surprised that we were practically raised together. Our personalities, outlook and attitude towards people and things and the results of our lives to date are totally different. Sharing the same family — our mothers are sisters — and the fact that we both attended the same primary school is where all the similarities ended. The reality was I had it constantly drilled into my head that the only way to make a better life for yourself and your family was to go to school, study hard and get a good job. My Auntie Ann, Toni's mother, did her best to help my mother and me whenever she could. She would buy me items of clothing and I remember her paying for my driving lessons and braces when I needed them. The truth is, when you have limited resources, you learn to persevere.

MAKE THE MOST OF
YOUR OPPORTUNITIES

Up until I was 11 years old, I had no real concept of money, class or wealth except to the extent that I was frequently told, "Eat all your food on that plate. Children in Africa have no food to eat." There was no other place that I had been to or no one I came into contact with up to that point in my life where the division of wealth was so stark than at secondary school.

Not everyone had money, but it was noticeable who had and who did not have. You could tell which students lived a lifestyle of comfort by the cars they were dropped off to school in, the latest sneakers they wore during our Physical Education classes and the discussions on where they had vacationed after taking the Barbados Secondary School Entrance Examination (BSSEE) or what is popularly known as the Common Entrance exam. It was in the classroom, though, that the playing field was levelled somewhat. It didn't matter who your parents were or where you came from. We had the same books, the same lessons, the same teachers and the same opportunity to listen and learn what was being taught.

I remember sitting in Form 1 at secondary school and our class teacher at the time asking us what we wanted to be when we grew up. I remember a girl in class, who I think left after either the first or second year to go to boarding school, declaring that when she grew up she wanted to marry a rich man so she wouldn't have to work. Can you imagine having such a single-minded focus of wanting to marry rich at such a young age? The rest of us didn't know any better (Ha! Ha! Ha!). We wanted to be doctors and lawyers and engineers and vets. After reading Barbadian novelist Austin 'Tom' Clarke's *Growing Up Stupid Under the Union Jack*, I wanted to be a writer. The book was a dazzling account of a boy's experience growing up in Barbados in the 1940s and highlighted how his mother struggled against insurmountable odds, yet succeeded in giving her son the best available education. In that moment I identified with Clarke's story and wanted to transport readers like he had transported me with his writing and to entertain them as well. But somehow along the way I was told to get a profession. "Writers are starving artists; they don't make much money. If you still want to write after getting your professional qualifications, do it then."

To whom much is given, much is expected. Because I recognised how much everyone was trying to help and the sacrifices they were making, I always felt like I had to excel; I had to be the best. What became clear was we have no say into what circumstances we are born, and it is pointless to complain. Our time would be better spent making the most of the opportunities we are given and trying to make something of our lives.

HOW I MET MY FATHER

I suppose the most poignant thing which happened in these years came at the end of my year in second form. I am still amazed that my mother actually let me out of her sight long enough to go, but I remember spending six glorious weeks in the U.S. on holiday. We, that is, my cousin Toni and I, travelled alone without the assistance of a hostess. I ate pizza slices which cost US$1 almost every day, went shopping on Flatbush and ate Italian ice.

I am amazed that even at the time of writing I can still remember the address by heart. This would have been my first time visiting Brooklyn and staying in a high-rise apartment but not Toni's first time; she was a seasoned traveller. In Barbados, most persons live in houses and the few apartment buildings that I knew of were never more than two or three storeys high, while Brooklyn's high-rise apartment buildings are twenty and thirty storeys in the air. Brooklyn was enveloped in this thick, sticky heat. I remember seeing lots of bars, restaurants, coffee shops and clothing stores along Flatbush. There were parks, but the place still had a dense urban feel. It was nothing like my surroundings in Barbados with its green grass, fruit trees, gentle breezes and generally calm feel. The place felt large, very large, and anywhere we walked I felt like I was walking forever. Everyone was hustling somewhere and spoke with an American twang, even the people who looked like they were from the Caribbean. It was also loud and noisy; every few minutes I could hear the siren of a police car, ambulance or fire engine wailing in the distance.

We stayed with Toni's father and other relatives from her father's side. She also had another aunt who had an apartment downstairs from us. We visited other family members and friends, sometimes nearby, sometimes in the Bronx or Queens. We went on bus rides to the Poconos, Atlantic City, the Amish Village and Chinatown. We visited the Statue of Liberty, Ellis Island, Coney Island and spent weeks on Long Island where Toni's grandmother worked. I especially loved when Toni's father, Uncle Andy, would take us out to Manhattan and Greenwich Village to see if we could spot any actors or actresses. I just remember tons and tons of laughter. We were having the time of our lives. This was by far my best vacation yet and I was drinking in the adventure and newness of the experience.

About a few weeks into the vacation, I was told by Toni's grandmother that my father was coming to collect me to spend the weekend at his house. Very interesting term, "my father", since I barely remembered him at that time and we barely spoke. He was largely absent from my life until this trip. At the age of 12 that is a rough thing to think about. A part of me really didn't want to go. Why should I be made to go? Why were we only now having this meeting when for years I had wondered what had become of him? Had he ever wondered about me? Why now when I had made it this far without him? Apparently, my mother had already discussed the possibility of me visiting my father with him and Toni's grandmother. He had his own family — a wife, a stepdaughter who was my age and my younger half-brother. I, of course, wondered how this weekend would be as I had replayed this moment over and over many times before. It was awkward for the most part.

My father lived in upstate New York at the time. It was totally different from Brooklyn where I had been staying with Toni and her grandmother. The houses were all neatly lined along the street and there were skunks and squirrels scampering across the perfectly manicured lawns. My father was living the life I had only read about in books and I felt like an outsider. My younger cousin and Toni's sister, Rhea, who was probably three or four years old at the time, made the journey with me upstate. She had just arrived in New York, three weeks into our vacation, and wanted to go upstate with me as she was close to my little brother Akeal's age and would have someone to play with. Everyone thought it was a splendid idea and it meant I wouldn't have to go alone with a group of strangers, because essentially that was what they were.

My father arrived in a black sedan with his family to collect me from Toni's grandmother's apartment. The drive was probably the longest I had ever experienced, and all I remember thinking on the drive there was how much I would miss Brooklyn. Rhea enjoyed herself with my stepsister and little brother, but she was at that very young age where having someone to play with was all that mattered. I, however, was a little older and I could tell that my stepmother and father were really trying. They ensured I had all the foods and snacks I liked. They took us to Rye Playland which was an amusement park not too far away and allowed us free range of the rides that included the bumper cars, the magic carpet ride, grand carousel and gondola wheel to our hearts' content.

I could tell from his relaxed and loving interactions with my stepsister that he had a great relationship with her even though she wasn't his blood daughter. All during my time there and up to the time I left, I was polite and displayed the manners that would make my mother and Auntie Ann proud. After all, they were the ones who worked hard on me.

YOU SURVIVE DESPITE
THE MADNESS

Somehow, I managed to survive all the madness that was secondary school and got through my university years by giving of my best. I was able to get through my years of both university and law school with the help of my aunt and by securing jobs to help me maintain myself and with a lot of help from my proverbial village and my tribe (great friends whom I met along the way who became my core group of people).

Once I had successfully completed law school in 2008, I managed to land myself a job where I had to work twice as hard as my male colleagues to prove that I had earned my place at the table. And so, when the opportunity arose, I worked two jobs; I worked from 7:30 a.m. to 3:30 p.m. in a private practice and then from 3:30 p.m. until about 10 p.m. I clocked more hours with another company. During those initial years after becoming an attorney-at-law I was intent on soaking up all the experience I could get. Even after all that sacrifice and years of studying, I knew I still could not afford to just rest on my laurels.

Eventually, however, my hard work did pay off and, in 2010, I joined the legal team of a large multinational company. I started out as the legal counsel covering nine markets in the Eastern Caribbean. When I was at law school, I had always envisioned myself in this type of role. After spending two years in private practice, I was delighted when I landed this in-house position. After my manager got a new and more exciting opportunity at a different company, I was promoted to legal and regulatory manager for the Eastern Caribbean, adding more of the regulatory function of nine markets to my legal remit as well. I was responsible for advising the C-suite and business units in those nine markets on any legal or regulatory matters that may arise during the course of business. There was never an opportunity to get bored.

Close to the beginning of my new role I got to travel to St. Lucia for a meeting with the regulator there. I was excited about that since it was my first work trip. Work was going really well. I enjoyed it so much that most days it didn't seem like work and I was pleased with my career progression thus far. Plus, I really liked those short trips out of the island. I was never keen about travelling on LIAT, our Caribbean regional airline, in the initial years, but I have since embraced it. Apart from the countless stops like a ZR in the sky, its flights were often hours late or cancelled altogether. LIAT — which originally stood for Leeward Island Air Transport — was so notorious for its bad service that over the years Caribbean folk came up with what we considered more appropriate meanings for its acronym. These included Leave Island Any Time and Luggage in Another Terminal (or Territory), even Lousy in All Things. However, during my unpleasant encounters with the airline and its flights I learnt that it was not the situation itself but how I responded to it. I tried to see the silver lining and took it as an opportunity to catch up on more work or some reading when these things happened. There was no use complaining anyway, and there wasn't much else to do in most of these island airports.

A RELATIONSHIP
TO NOWHERE

As I was getting ready for my trip to St. Lucia, I got a call from someone at the University of the West Indies (UWI), Cave Hill campus who informed me that I came 3rd in their inaugural 6K and had won a cash prize of BDS$100. At first I thought it was a joke, but, as it turned out, I did place 3rd in the race with a time of 40:41, having walked at some points along the course. Naturally, I was pretty excited, and, in a moment of weakness, I emailed William to let him know.

William was my sometimes...I don't even have a name for it. He and I met one evening several years ago in Second Street, Holetown. My friend and I had walked into a restaurant while he was sitting by the bar area. Upon seeing us, he immediately got up and bravely came over to where we were, declared that he would like to date me and gave me his card. I thought he was intoxicated and I found the entire encounter very hilarious. After a couple weeks or so I was cleaning out my handbag and found the card he had given me. On a whim, I gave him a call and he invited me to dinner at the Lone Star Restaurant, a chic fine-dining restaurant located on the west coast of the island not very far from where we had initially met. After that dinner, we went out for a movie, then another evening to a play at UWI, on another occasion to the beach and, before I knew it, we were dating. Two years later I learnt that William had commitment issues and we were in a relationship to nowhere, so I had previously deleted him from my Blackberry. This email, of course, reopened the communication line and he took this opportunity to tell me that he missed me. I had missed seeing him also and, in that moment, I gave in and told him I would love to see him on the weekend, although I was not sure I would be able to because of my impending trip.

I hesitate to use the word "relationship" when it comes to William, but whether I want to admit it or not, in reality, it was a relationship, albeit a dysfunctional one. "Dysfunctional" is probably not the best word because we both functioned really well within the parameters of this "relationship". We were blissfully happy when we saw each other and we would often have dinner at our favourites: The Cliff, Lone Star and Daphne's. We never argued and always had a perfect time together. I suppose it worked. I didn't stress him, and he didn't stress me. The problem, I suppose, was that I wanted more — the commitment, the marriage, the house...everything — and it became clear to me over the years that he didn't. I used to feel guilty about wanting it all, but why shouldn't we want it all? Society tells us we can have it all and then makes us feel guilty for wanting it all. There is absolutely nothing wrong with wanting more.

The final nail in the coffin that was our dodgy relationship came about a year later in December 2013 when William forgot my birthday and not for the first time in our almost four years together. I mean, how difficult was it to remember that my birthday is December 31? It is one of the easiest days in the year to remember, so that this upset me is totally justifiable. I had ghosted him several times in the past, but somehow I knew that this newest stunt had done irreparable damage to our "relationship". I had had enough. It was time to move on. There comes a point when you have to say that enough is enough and realise your worth. I told him sometime back that he should get professional help for his commitment issues and I had come to the realisation that if he wanted professional help he would get it. He could certainly afford it. I was tired of what we were doing, and it was starting to have an effect on me. I had to be strong and realise that there was nothing wrong with me. I kept constantly hearing these words in my head: *You are smart enough to know that there is no future in this.* I needed to heed those words.

TIME FOR A CHANGE
OF SCENERY

Wednesday, May 21, 2014

I leave next Wednesday. I can hardly believe any of it. I had been feeling restless for some time and in need of a change.

The opportunity came in the form of an email one day as I sat at my desk at work. The email was sent by the General Counsel in the Pacific markets asking for someone to come to assist in Myanmar for three months and I was asked if I was interested by the Group General Counsel who also advised me to think long and hard about the assignment. However, I didn't feel I needed to give it too much thought, so I just said yes. I felt as though this was the answer to the restlessness I had been experiencing lately. I was asked how soon I could be ready and, wanting to keep things clean and simple, I said June 1.

Truth is, I didn't know what I would possibly need to get ready. I have no kids or husband to make provisions for, so this was the perfect time to go. It made no sense to me to delay things. In my experience, the longer you ponder over things, the more time you have to come up with several reasons why you shouldn't do something. As part of my preparation, I searched the internet for all I could find on Myanmar. I had been made aware of the place back in 2012 when it was beginning to open up to the rest of the world for tourism, for investments, for everything really. Home to over 51 million people and 135 officially recognised ethnic groups, Myanmar had previously been closed off from the rest of the world and ruled with an iron hand by the military.

Why the hell not? It will be something to put on my CV. I have been with this company for four years now and getting a bit tired of it all, so I need to be thinking about what's next. It will soon be my seventh anniversary of being called to the Bar. The irony of this entire thing is that another major company called me the day before I was preparing to leave for London (the first leg of my trip to Myanmar) and was inquiring about my availability for an interview on June 13, 2014 for a position. I had to tell them that I had already accepted a secondment to Myanmar. I hoped that this was not a mistake, but I wanted to see another part of the world and what better way to do this.

This will be my first time to South East Asia and being so far away from home. The furthest I was from home was Paris in April 2012 for a two-week holiday and that is only an eight-hour flight to Gatwick, London and then a 2-hour-and-28-minute ride on the Eurostar from London St. Pancras International to Paris Gare du Nord. This would be different. This was not a holiday. The journey to Yangon, Myanmar would be a whopping eight-hour flight to London, a car ride to change from Gatwick to Heathrow, 13 hours and 37 minutes to Malaysia and three hours to Yangon. I had been praying for a change and God sent this.

PART THREE

MYANMAR

A Unique Experience in Yangon

SOMEWHERE BETWEEN LONDON AND KUALA LUMPUR

Friday, May 30, 2014

Cillian didn't believe in God. I met Cillian in 2012 while in Jamaica on a work trip. After our intense days of training, we would hang out by the pool of the Courtleigh Hotel where we were staying to relax, unwind and talk about anything that came into our heads. He was raised Catholic in a working-class Irish family, but he no longer believed. I don't know how he couldn't believe.

As I sit here flying to Kuala Lumpur, the capital city of Malaysia, I ask myself how could God not exist. I look out the window and it is dark now and the vast darkness suddenly makes me think of the scripture in the Book of Genesis in the Bible which speaks about God creating the world out of nothing. That scripture speaks about how the earth was formless and empty and darkness was over the face of the earth. However, when God said, "Let there be light" light appeared. It reminds me also that the God who created the entire world cared about a young woman from a small island so much that he would answer my prayer for change by providing me with this opportunity.

When you are situated in only one part of the world, it is easy to underestimate the sheer vastness and wonder of the earth sometimes. I am watching *Mandela: Long Walk to Freedom* as my inflight movie and I think to myself that this is probably not the best idea because it makes me angry and sad at the same time and these are not emotions I want to feel now. I should be buzzing with joy and excitement on this second leg of my journey to Myanmar (the first leg was Barbados to London), but I continue to keep it on as I write this. It stirs up some great emotions in me. I want to cry; it makes me think of home and of my family and of the oppression of black people. I am angry but most of all it is a poignant reminder of who I am. As I embark on this journey to commence my secondment as legal manager for the legal team in Myanmar, I think I will need to remind myself of who I am. Sometimes it is easy to forget when you get caught up in the busyness of life. When you remember who you are, you interact with the world on a different level.

I had asked for time to write, to see the world and for some quiet. Yangon should give me all these things. I thank God as I sit here in an otherwise empty row on the plane looking out into the darkness. I do not think that this is a mere coincidence. Why do I want to go to this place? All I know of Yangon is information I had found on the internet, which is largely outdated, and from the information pack which my company sent me when I accepted this assignment. Ironically, the company's information pack, although well put together, is filled with the same outdated details I sourced online. Am I terrified? Yes! Am I excited? Yes! I look forward to all Yangon has to offer.

It had been a crazy few days leading up to this journey. I had to visit my doctor and get all types of shots which were recommended by my company before I flew into Myanmar. I had to make a detailed list of matters my Auntie Ann should look after for me while I was away, such as starting my car every few days, letting the townhouse where I lived get some air so the dust won't build up and checking the mailbox. I also gave her account details to make online bill payments on my behalf since I wasn't entirely sure what the internet situation would be like in Myanmar once I got there. I had to prepare detailed handover notes for the matters I was handling at the local office for my manager just in case anything came up. Though he would be able to reach me via email, there was the time difference to consider and he may need to respond to his own manager urgently. When I did my layover in London before I boarded this second-leg flight to Malaysia, I had entertained the thought of making a run for it. I have always liked London and it is a great gateway to the rest of Europe. That I had only completed the first leg of my journey and had already had an eight-hour flight, plus a switch of airports from Gatwick to Heathrow was taking a toll on me. This journey to Myanmar is the most gruelling I have ever experienced. The reality of how far I will be away from home and how alone I truly am is now sinking in. What if I didn't turn up for the secondment? What if I just disappeared in London and kept going?

KUALA LUMPUR, MALAYSIA

Saturday, May 31, 2014

I left Barbados since Tuesday evening, got to London on Wednesday morning, took a car from Gatwick to Heathrow and slept over in London at Sofitel, Heathrow on Wednesday night. On Thursday morning at around 11 a.m. I left London and my flight touched down at Kuala Lumpur International Airport, Malaysia at around 7:30 a.m. yesterday.

I didn't think Malaysia would be such a modern place. As the driver transported me from the airport to the hotel room yesterday morning, I was surprised by the number of skyscrapers and the amount of construction that is going on. We passed a lot of coconut trees which reminded me that I am still in a tropical country. If I had to compare it to a Caribbean island, I would say that Malaysia reminds me a lot of Trinidad. The highway was chock-a-block with cars and vehicles of every type. The drive from the airport took close to two hours to reach the hotel. As we neared the Kuala Lumpur City Centre (KLCC), I could see why it is the heart of Kuala Lumpur (KL) and why people have referred to Malaysia as Asia's New York — the city is buzzing with activity.

I am amazed by the view of the Petronas Towers — the world's largest twin towers. I can understand why Natasha, a schoolmate of mine from my secondary school days, would choose to live here. It would be nice to meet up with her, I muse, but I have no idea how to get in contact with her or if she even lives near my hotel. Malaysia is a massive place and she may not even be in KL at all. In any case, I am only in KL for one day to get my business visa for Myanmar and continue on my way. It all happened so quickly that I didn't have time to contact her mother who works at the university in Barbados and ask for her contact details. It has been a long time since I have spoken to Nat. I am not even sure if she is still in Malaysia.

Before I left Barbados, Anthony, my running partner, told me these were places he had only read about in Geography books and he was a little jealous that I was getting to see them. Logan, a colleague, texted me a little while ago for an update on where I am. I actually like Logan sometimes, mostly when he is not harassing me about work. He has this habit of calling me after six on evenings to ask me something about work. I think there should be a policy of no work-related questions after 6 p.m. unless it is urgent, but everything is always urgent, so invariably I end up working long hours and on the weekends. He said I should enjoy the first impressions. Indeed, I intend to enjoy the entire experience.

Yesterday morning was probably the most anxious I have been on the entire trip. I had to present myself at the Myanmar Embassy in Malaysia for a business visa. If I didn't get this visa, I couldn't fly to Myanmar today and I would miss my Monday start date for my secondment. Business visas for Myanmar are processed in Malaysia or Thailand. Malaysia was easier for me since the Thailand route would have required me to fly to New York first to get a visa for Thailand and then get a visa for Myanmar once I reached Thailand. Apparently, Myanmar has very strict rules regarding visas there. A valid visa must be shown at the airport and at the hotel, and security checkpoints are common outside the tourist areas. Tourists are not even allowed in some states. Certain business travellers can get a visa on arrival, but since I have a Barbados passport, I have to do it the long way.

Yesterday, after I cleared my luggage in Malaysia, I purchased a taxi coupon and placed myself on the sidewalk for a taxi to take me to the hotel. I read online that I should do this to avoid the queue and that it eliminates the need to pay cash at the end of the journey and having to deal with touts. Anything to make my life easier after a 13-hour flight. My young taxi driver wanted to know where I was from, and when I said Barbados his eyes lit up. He said, "You mean in the Caribbean?" and he starts to sing "Umbrella". I suppose I have Rihanna to thank for more people now knowing of Barbados. I have to say, all in all, I find the people in Kuala Lumpur to be very friendly and for that I am grateful.

I was under the assumption that they would accept US dollars here, but when I went to put down my bags at the hotel and asked about getting to the Myanmar Embassy, the hotel concierge told me that they don't. I didn't have a choice but to leave the hotel and find a money changer to get local currency to pay for my visa, agency fees and taxi drivers. It was too early to check into the hotel as it is only just after 9 a.m. The concierge gave me a map of KLCC and circled the money changer on it. He also pointed me in the direction I should walk. I walked for a few metres and paused to study the map, but it all looked like gibberish. I had never developed the skill of learning to read maps as intricate as this one, or any map for that matter. I was frustrated and so very close to throwing an adult tantrum, but I knew it would be futile. I was under a great time deadline. Plus, I had to keep my wits about me in this new place. Suddenly, and as if on cue, a slightly chubby Malaysian girl with long black hair to her waist whom I hadn't noticed before asked me if I was lost. She was dressed like a student, in jeans and running shoes and was carrying a red backpack. I told her I was looking for a money changer and she said she would show me as she was walking in that direction. However, when we got there, it wasn't open. Apparently, that particular money changer opened at 11 a.m., but there was no way I could wait until then as valuable time was running out and I had to get my visa before the close of business. I needed to find another money changer. I walked along the underground tunnel of Kuala Lumpur City Centre (KLCC) that the Malaysian girl showed me. It was much like the underground in New York with various shops, except there was security every few meters and it was way cleaner than New York. Thankfully I didn't get lost that time, but I couldn't help but think of what a colossal waste of time this was turning out to be. I needed to get to the embassy. I suppose it didn't help that I had just come off a 13-hour flight and was very tired and slightly miserable and all I wanted was to shower and throw myself onto the clean white sheets of my hotel bed.

However, it would be a while before I got to be anywhere near my hotel room. After getting the local currency at the money changer and exiting the underground, I was able to hail a taxi and explain to him where I wanted to go. Perhaps he didn't understand my instructions since he took me to the wrong location. When I got there, lots of Asians were sitting in what seemed like a backyard on benches which was located next to a white building. Someone pointed me straight to the window of a building across the yard and then the guy there sent me to the last window. When I told the girl at the window I wanted an express business visa she said they didn't do them there and gave me a piece of paper with directions. *Breathe! Breathe!* I kept telling myself. Precious time was being wasted. Luckily, the first taxi driver who brought me to this wrong backyard location only charged six Malaysian dollars. From here, I got my second taxi driver, Li, who took me to the right agency. He charged me twenty Malaysian dollars, though. I didn't even know what the exchange rate was to the US dollar and I didn't really care at this point. I felt he was ripping me off, but I had no way of knowing, short of asking him, because there was no meter running. Besides, I liked him, and I got the impression that he was hustling to make money for his family.

What made me nervous was that I had to leave my passport at that place. You never realise how much you rely on that little document until you have to part with it for any length of time. How lost you can feel without it, especially when outside of your home country. Suppose these people packed up and moved shop? How the hell would I get out of Malaysia? I suppose if there were Barbados embassies or consulates around the nervousness would have subsided. The nearest consulates we have are in China and an honorary consulate in Singapore. Neither issues passports.

After what seemed like hours of waiting, I eventually got the visa and made it back to the hotel. It is funny how hotel rooms temporarily become homes. On the ride back to Traders Hotel, which is located right in the heart of the Kuala Lumpur City Centre (KLCC) and opposite the Suria KLCC shopping mall with the Petronas Twin Towers and the KLCC Park nearby, the taxi driver haggled me non-stop. After such a hectic round-about day I enjoyed having a little fun with him and I started to relax as I had accomplished the goal of getting my visa and I was no longer under time constraints and feeling pressured.

The taxi driver, who looked to be in his early twenties at the most, was a boss driver, weaving in and out through Malaysian traffic. I got back to the hotel and checked in as it was well after 3 p.m. by then, collected my room keys from Reception and headed to my room which is fantastic. It is spacious, clean and inviting. Did I mention the amazing view of the Petronas Towers? The Towers have 88 floors each and are joined at the 41st and 42nd floor. I can see why it is described as one of the world's most iconic engineering feats. I was in awe and I did what any self-respecting human would do — I took a quick selfie of myself with the towers in the background. #Blessed.

From my room, I could also see Lake Symphony with its colourful light fountain and the KLCC Park below. The 13-hour flight and waiting around on my passport had taken a toll on me, but I was also very excited about the journey I was about to embark upon. As I sat in my well-appointed hotel room just after returning from the hassle of sorting out my visa, a part of me wished I was staying in Malaysia longer and not travelling on to Myanmar so quickly. I wished I wasn't so tired so that maybe I could take in a little more of Malaysia, but I could not deny that I was exhausted, so I showered and went to sleep.

I woke up around 1:15 this morning feeling better now that I had rested, and contemplated whether to go to Sky Bar on the 33rd floor of the hotel. I decided that I would as I may never get the chance again. Who knew if I would even make it out of Yangon? I went to Sky Bar at 2 a.m. and paused for a moment to take it in. The ceilings were high and there was a huge rectangular pool down the middle and couches all around. The bar was packed with patrons despite the hour. It all looked very lush and posh. I could feel the gentle breeze from the open windows and see all the lights from the surrounding skyscrapers. Yangon will probably be nothing like this. I met a couple KL guys who tried to dance with me. One of them mentioned to me that he visits Sky Bar every Friday, but I was not impressed. I would probably get tired going to the same place every Friday. I also met a couple Nigerian guys. Boy, Nigerians make it all over. I sat in one of the booths for a while and observed my surroundings. There was some great energy here. The bar closes at 3 a.m. and I made my exit just before then. The Nigerians were getting a little too close for comfort since they moved nearer to where I was seated. I got a few hours' sleep and woke up at 6 a.m. to shower and get ready.

My flight is at 11:00 a.m. so I need to leave the hotel by 8 a.m. to get to the airport and check in. At breakfast I realise Asians eat all kinds of things to start their day, even sushi. I leave the sushi alone, even though I am a big fan of California rolls. After breakfast I call our family friend Carlton. He has been on my mind. He retired at 35 and has travelled extensively. He used to regale me with stories of his travels to Iraq, Brussels, Devon and Cornwall among others — he hasn't been to Myanmar, though — and I credit him for igniting the travel bug in me. He is such a humorous person and I know that this phone call will surely make me laugh. We haven't spoken in a while and I didn't get the chance to tell him that I would be in Myanmar for three months. We have a pleasant chat and I am reminded of how much I miss him. We make a date to see each other on my return to Barbados. I feel a pang of sadness as I put down the phone. There is a 12-hour time difference between Barbados and KL, so while it is already Saturday morning here in KL it is still Friday night in Barbados.

I also miss my best friend Keisha — or Keis, for short — dearly. My conversation with Carlton has left me feeling a little homesick. It must have been the combination of the hellish day I had yesterday and knowing that I am absolutely alone in a new country. I pick up my phone to call Keis but then remember that it wouldn't have been a good time. It was the beginning of June and therefore the beginning of our Crop Over season in Barbados. I knew at that very moment Keis was at the Baje Crop Over band launch. I had forgotten about that, to be honest. She had been looking forward to it for months and was excited that her cousin got her into the VIP area.

FIRST IMPRESSIONS

Later on Saturday, May 31, 2014

Nothing at all could have prepared me for Myanmar. Absolutely nothing. I fly over and see the vast magical kingdom of what I think is Bagan, Myanmar. The view is breathtaking. Imagine a spacious, dusty plain with very few trees and about 2,000 pagodas as far as the eye can see. The temples dotted across the landscape are beautiful and I make a mental note that I must visit this part of the country before I leave Myanmar.

Immigration and customs are not as bad as I had read on the internet, which had made the process sound very convoluted. It is actually a breeze. Actually, it is a lot less threatening than immigration and customs in the U.S. I hand my Customs Declaration form in and move through the group of waiting agents and hotel representatives with name boards. Once that hurdle is over, I exit the airport where I search the crowd for Adam, my colleague who had sent me an email to say that he would meet me at the airport and to look for the guy with the red hair. I thought that was pretty nice of him. Even though I have travelled to several islands in the Caribbean on a regular basis for work, the only people ever greeting me were the company drivers. The heat of the place hits me and I peel off the cardigan I had been wearing on the plane. The crowd is a mass of people with taxi drivers in longyis (skirts) trying to get your attention, loved ones hugging each other and shouting out their names to get their attention. I have never met Adam before and have no idea what he looks like except that he said he has red hair. How many red-haired guys could there possibly be in Yangon? Then I see this tall, slim guy with red hair step from behind the crowd and wave to me. He is a slight little fellow but very tall. He looks like a giant compared to the tiny Burmese. Adam makes his way over to me and greets me with a smile.

"Hello, I am Adam. You must be Nadia. Nice to meet you." I detect what seems to be a New Zealand accent, but I can't be sure.

I tell him that it was nice to meet him as well and I thank him for meeting me at the airport. We walk towards the area with the taxis while a porter trails us pushing a trolley packed high with my luggage. We manage to load my large and extremely heavy suitcase into the taxi followed by my smaller carry-on and then we are off. I had to pack for three months, after all, even though it was my best friend Keis who really did my packing since I loathe packing. Once we are in the car Adam starts chatting excitedly.

"How was your flight?" he begins his string of questions, angling his body a little so that he is facing me instead of the back of our driver's head. "What route did you take to get here? How many days were you travelling?"

I am exhausted from my trip, but it feels good to have a meaningful conversation with someone and I am excited to have made it to my final destination. "It was good. Uneventful. The flight from London to Malaysia on Malaysia Airlines was practically empty," I report. "I flew Barbados to London, changed airports, London to Kuala Lumpur and then Kuala Lumpur to Yangon. I left Barbados since Tuesday; it took me five days to get here."

Adam is in awe at the distance I have travelled to be here. His own trip to Yangon was only one 11-hour flight. Along the way, Adam points out the various outdoor markets where Burmese people shop for their fruits, vegetables and household items. He tells me that they sell all manner of things at these roadside markets and shops.

"You seem to know a lot about the place," I comment as I take in all of the new knowledge like a good student and make a mental note of the various places so that I can visit them once I have settled.

"Yes, I am learning. I have been here about three weeks. I flew over from Melbourne where I have been living and working but I am from New Zealand."

"Oh, a Kiwi. I heard New Zealand is lovely. Will your family be joining you?"

"Yes, yes, New Zealand *is* lovely," Adam confirms, nodding his head. "You should definitely visit one day. I don't have my own family yet, but my parents are still in New Zealand. My girlfriend lives in Melbourne and she is also a lawyer. She got an amazing opportunity to work for an airline company and I got this amazing opportunity to be here in Myanmar."

He says they will see how it goes. He doesn't seem convinced that the relationship will last the separation and neither am I. I am not a huge believer in long distance relationships. I remember how much André (my first real boyfriend) and I grew apart when I was away at law school. It had huge implications for our relationship afterwards and our subsequent break up. I do recall that I had asked him to move to Trinidad to be with me while I was at law school, but he didn't because he didn't think he would have found a job in Trinidad and a myriad of other excuses so I shouldn't feel guilty for what happened after that. Relationships are hard enough as it is without the added complications of distance. I suppose in hindsight it was good that he hadn't joined me in Trinidad. We had been together from the time I was about nineteen and there were times when I wasn't certain where he began and where I ended. It was probably good that I had a chance to grow and be on my own.

As we make our way to our hotel, Adam is silent as he gazes through the window and I take the opportunity to soak in the sights. Yangon is not at all like New York, Paris, London or even Kuala Lumpur. There are crumbling old buildings dating back to the colonial period. It was like taking a step back in time in a frozen time capsule. Driving through the streets reminded me of what I have seen on TV of the slums of Brazil — a crisscross of low-hanging electricity wires overhead, open sewers, laundry hanging out on the rusted wrought iron balconies, boys in the street playing a ball game and balls of barbed wire on imposing gates protecting the properties behind them — except we weren't in South America, we were in South East Asia. In fact, Myanmar was the poorest country in South East Asia. I think to myself my L.K.Bennett flats, Jorge Bischoff designer shoes and Michael Kors and Longchamp bags really have no place here. I began to wish I had told Keisha to pack differently. I often justify these purchases by saying that I will get my money's worth from the usage. I feel guilty now, though, knowing that the cost of these items could probably feed families for weeks or longer.

After a little while, I ask, "How is the office? What is it like?"

"The office is a riot. You will be managing a team of local lawyers, and their English is not very good," he says with a chuckle. He must have seen the slightly puzzled expression on my face, because he quickly adds, "But don't worry. There is a translator who sits in the Legal Department. They are an eager bunch. They wrote their names out on their desks for you so you can learn them easily. They have chatted about your arrival all week and are excited that you are joining the team. Everyone is around our age — mid 20s to early 30s. Because the country has been closed off for so long, their confidence levels are low, but it will get better over time."

Somehow, as Adam explains some of the dynamics in the office, I begin to get even more excited about this new work adventure in

Yangon. "Thanks for this insight, Adam. I can't wait to meet them."

The ride to the hotel was pleasant enough. I decide right away that I like Adam. He seems genuine and down to earth.

The hotel is just okay, and I have stayed in lots of hotels. There is no swimming pool for cooling off on hot days or executive lounge to escape the regular paying guests which you sometimes need on business trips. I have a phobia when it comes to hotels for the first few days of my stay. Perhaps it is my Auntie Ann's insistence on bringing her own sheets to put on top of the hotel sheets and pillowcases when we travelled when I was younger. And back then these were five-star hotels. It is only as I got older that I realised how ludicrous it was and that these extra linens were taking up valuable real estate in my suitcase and adding to the weight limit in free baggage allowance for airlines.

At the hotel in Yangon, instead of a view of the Petronas Towers, I get a view of the trash heap. The building next to the hotel which I can see out my window is pretty dilapidated, but I later learn that what I thought was a dilapidated building where people dump trash is really a monastery. I will request to be moved, perhaps tomorrow, and to a room with a nicer view, hopefully. But right now, I am still a bit tired from the long flights and multiple time zones. I try to cast my reservations about hotel rooms from my mind and I busy myself with getting ready for bed. Just as I am doing that, I swear I see bugs crawling out of the chairs and the couch. Maybe I am imagining things because I am so tired. It seems I will be here for a while, so I have to make myself comfortable and try to enjoy myself.

* * *

The Skype call to Keisha to let her know that I made it to Yangon safely so that she could let my family know was a disaster; the call kept freezing because of the poor Wi-Fi connection. We could barely finish our sentences before there was a freeze and then one of us would have to disconnect and call back. Between the many interruptions, she was able to tell me about the Baje band launch. She says the costumes cost US$300 and I cannot help but think how many people that US$300 could feed here.

So far, I have briefly met two other expats outside the hotel whom Adam introduced me to as he and the taxi driver were unloading my bags from the car — Noah, who is from New Zealand but lived in Melbourne just like Adam, and Evan from the UK. Noah is in site acquisition while Evan is in construction. When I think about expats, Noah seems like the typical image that comes to mind — here to make some money and drink some beer. The beer costs only 2000 kyats (or K2,000) which is US$2. Kyats is the official currency of Myanmar.

Maybe I will fall in love with Yangon, who knows. It is early days yet.

A VISIT TO SHWEDAGON PAGODA AND THE STRAND

Sunday, June 1, 2014

My body has not yet adjusted to the time zones. After sleeping the entire of last night away, I arise early and unpack a few things, mostly my toiletries. Keisha had packed three months' worth of toiletries so my suitcases were very heavy.

While it is 5:58 a.m. on Sunday here, it is still only 3:28 p.m. on Saturday in Barbados — a whopping 10-hour-and-30-minute time difference. Keisha and my friend and travel buddy Nicole call me as they are liming at Keisha's townhouse watching Anthony Bourdain's *Parts Unknown — Myanmar* back in Barbados. They warn me off the train ride and the tea shops. Apparently, the rides are not for the faint of heart and should only be undertaken if you are a daring thrill-seeker. The trains are dirty and uncomfortable as most of them are outdated. Since people are allowed to bring livestock on the train, the seats and aisles are scuffed and stained, and don't even think about using the bathrooms. The overall ride can be extremely jolting regardless of if you purchase an ordinary class ticket, first class ticket or upper-class ticket. As for the local tea shops, they serve super sweet tea, but Keis and Nic say my stomach may not be able to take the water that the tea is made with. In terms of communicating in these local tea shops, I may be able to get by with gestures, but I will pretty much have to figure out the menu on my own.

It is hilarious. They seem very concerned that I would choose to come to Myanmar. As I chat with them, I remember that it was only the Saturday before I left for Yangon that I was having lunch with Nicole and her mother on the south coast of the island at Bert's Bar. I miss Bert's Bar now. After they have made all their jokes and are finished being animated, Nicole tells me that it was very brave of me to embark on this journey in Yangon.

I am booked at this hotel for a month to start. It is not a bad hotel, but I can't see myself living at a hotel for a month. It is clean at least, in a good location, the lobby and dining areas are nice enough and there is 24-hour room service. Maybe it is the green paint that throws me off. I am not a fan of green, and the brown and beige does little to lift the atmosphere. Little did I know at the time that I would have ended up living at that hotel for the full three months of my stay in Yangon.

I have always been an early riser; my grandmother instilled that in me from young. Even when I was an adult living alone, she would ring me early to make sure I was out of bed. I liked getting up early; it gives you more hours in the day to get things done. I have made up my mind that I will visit the Shwedagon Pagoda today to see what all the hype is about. Every single article I read online said it was a must-see in Yangon.

After I finish my chat with Nic and Keis, I get ready and head down to breakfast where I meet Khing, my Burmese waiter, for the first time. Khing is slim with cropped black hair and a brown complexion and looks like he could be in his 20s. As he is taking my order, he asks me where I am from. I tell him I am from Barbados and he is very friendly and helpful. He tells me there is a Jamaican staying at the hotel as well. I can tell he takes great pride in his work by the way he speaks to me and handles the other guests who enter the dining room for breakfast.

He inquires if this is my first time in Myanmar and when I tell him yes, he encourages me to go out and see the place.

Before I got to Yangon, I read that the banking system is not very good, so I travelled here with a stack of cash and hoped for the best. After breakfast I visit the hotel reception desk and change US$50 to kyats which amounts to about 49,500 kyats (or K49,500) — they keep K500 for their trouble of making the exchange — and I go upstairs to change my shirt since I read somewhere that sleeveless shirts are not allowed in the Shwedagon Pagoda. The girl at the front desk gives me a card with the address and a small map with directions to the hotel on it so I can get back after exploring. I am on my way. I pass the lake and park which Adam had told me about on the ride from the airport. I may take a walk there later in the evening, I thought, or perhaps not. Who was I kidding? One excursion was enough for me for one day. As I gaze out of the window, the taxi driver asks if I am married and I tell him that I am not. This is the first of many times I would be asked this question while in Myanmar. I wonder why he would ask me that question, but I have arrived at the magnificent Shwedagon Pagoda, which is also known as the Golden Pagoda, and I don't give it much more thought. On later reflection, I think I should have asked him in jest if he wanted to marry me, but he may not have understood that I was only joking. I didn't want any trouble before my secondment even started. Maybe it was a bit strange for him to see a young woman travelling alone.

He drops me off at the south entrance for foreigners. I am a foreigner here. It is a massive place. There are groups with tour guides as well as solo visitors, like myself, and families. There is a long line being manned by four girls. Even though I have already taken off my slippers and placed them in my bag, one of the four girls working at the entrance tells me I have to leave my shoes. Hopefully no one takes them, I think to myself, and I leave them in the area designated for shoes. She tells me the entrance fee, places a green sticker on me to show I am a foreigner and insists that I leave K2,000 to rent a longyi. I think my skirt is modest enough, but I leave the K2,000 for the longyi anyway because I want to enter. She ties a green one around me to match my green foreigner sticker. I take the elevator up and nothing prepares me for the opulence and magnificence I see. There are huge Buddha statues and people praying and lighting candles and chanting. The Pagoda is built of gold. The stupa's plinth is made of bricks covered with genuine gold plates and the main stupa itself is entirely covered in gold, with a crowning umbrella encrusted with diamonds and other jewels. I have never seen anything like it and I am amazed. That the country could be so poor but there standing is this golden pagoda in the midst of it pays homage to the importance of Buddhism to Myanmar which is 99% Buddhist. I remember it is Sunday and I think to myself that maybe visiting the Golden Pagoda and praying as many were doing is like going to church to them. The ground is blazing hot by now and burning my feet, even though it isn't yet 10 a.m. I walk around and pay a local US$2 (K2,000) to take some pictures of me with my own camera. He happily obliges.

When I have had enough of the pagoda, I take the elevator back down. I purchase the longyi for an additional K5,000 because I like it so much and take a taxi back to my hotel to escape the heat. Once back in my room, I upload the pics to Facebook and email a few to myself. Since my trip to London back in 2008 where my bag was stolen, I learnt that I must take the photos off the camera quickly in case my bag with my camera in it gets stolen again and all my precious photos are lost. Adam had also suggested visiting the market, but I have three months here after all and don't want to do everything in one day and then be bored of the place. I will take my time to discover Myanmar.

I have a quick nap before I am awakened by housekeeping at about 12.30 p.m. They have come to clean the room. The little Burmese boy who is about to clean the room takes off his shoes, bows and enters. I call him a boy because they all look very young here and I can't figure out his age, but he could have been of the legal age to work. I leave him to it and go and sit in the hotel lobby where I see Khing. He stops to say hello and I cannot help but ask him why the Burmese boy who came to clean my room took off his shoes and bowed before he entered. He says that it is normal for them to bow as it is a sign of respect. He further explains that Burmese people take off their shoes when entering someone's home also as a sign of respect and because shoes are very dirty and since the hotel room is my home he wouldn't walk through my home with dirty shoes. He also tells me that poor boys from the countryside come to the city and take these housekeeping jobs to make a better life for themselves and their family. I am getting a soft spot for Khing. I tell him I just came back from the Shwedagon Pagoda and show him the picture of me in a longyi. He says I look beautiful. He is so kind. I was going to wait until 2 p.m. to eat, but I decide I am hungry now and I walk with Khing to the hotel restaurant. After I am seated, Khing tells me what is good on the menu and I order the Thai fried rice with no chicken and some tonic water with no ice and a slice of lemon to garnish. I read that the ice cubes are made with tap water so it was best to avoid them. The meal is enjoyable and Khing is very attentive. Even though he is busy he returns to my table several times to ask if everything is okay and whether I need anything else or would like some more tonic water. I am impressed by the service. I think that Khing could teach a few of the Western cultures a thing or two about excellence in customer service.

I go back up to my room and think about what to do next when I receive a call from the front desk. It is Adam who is also staying at the hotel. He is heading out but wants to make plans for dinner later. I happily accept. I am amazed at how exciting it is to get a call on the phone when you are in an unfamiliar country. It helps you to remember that you are not so alone after all. There is no international roaming here yet so I doubt I will be getting many calls since without international roaming it is impossible to make and receive international calls. The company I work for hopes to help in changing that. It wants to see Myanmar properly connected to the rest of the world. I have been seconded from the Eastern Caribbean to a telecommunications infrastructure business which is the newest business in the group of companies. I have to wait until I go to the office and get a local phone and SIM before I would be able to make and accept local calls. My smartphone won't work here since it has a micro SIM and only the regular SIMs are available. In any event, my phone isn't unlocked, so other than Blackberry messenger, WhatsApp, Instagram and Facebook, which I use sporadically due to temperamental Wi-Fi networks, I am pretty cut off. It doesn't bother me yet. The isolation may be good. Myanmar and my connectivity situation here remind me of Gabriel García Márquez's *One Hundred Years of Solitude*, except I will only be here roughly 90 days. In the book, the town has no contact with the outside world except for gypsies who occasionally visit but eventually loses its innocent and solitary state when it establishes contact with other towns in the region.

It is 6:55 p.m. and I head downstairs to meet Adam for our 7 p.m. dinner plans. I take the stairs because I have figured out that the Wi-Fi connection is lost once you enter the elevator. The electricity has also gone off a few times since I have been here, and I would hate to be trapped in the elevator, so I think I will try to take the stairs as often as possible.

We meet in the hotel lobby and he tells me that we have two options: some outdoor place up the road in the direction of the park or downtown. I choose downtown because I haven't been yet. The footman at the hotel whistles for a taxi for us and one promptly arrives. Adam tells the driver we are going to Chinatown, but I am sceptical, so I ask if he has been to The Strand yet. We go to The Strand instead and have dinner and great convo in the café there. The Strand Hotel is beautiful. It is a Victorian-style hotel and very quiet. It is easy to tell that it used to be a pompous display of wealth and might in colonial times since it still oozed of a colonial atmosphere. As we step inside, we are greeted with palm trees, marble floors, wicker chairs and gently swirling fans. Our waiter's English is impeccable. During the colonial period, The Strand was one of the most luxurious hotels in the British Empire with a clientele of exclusively whites. Coming from Barbados where, because of our colonial past, there were also places that were "exclusively white", this historical fact about The Strand does not escape me. Our family friend Carlton used to joke all the time when we attended polo matches in Barbados that it reminded him of apartheid in South Africa.

The hotel is listed on the Yangon City Heritage List. I read that, since the beginning, it was regarded as "the finest hostelry east of the Suez" and "patronised by royalty, nobility and distinguished personages". George Orwell spent time there when he was writing *Burmese Days*. Adam mentions that one of our colleagues lives here and I am jealous. As we eat, Adam and I talk about his work in Melbourne, the places we have travelled to, the ones still on our bucket lists and his time in Myanmar so far. This is not his first time in Myanmar; he had taken a year off to travel a while back and Myanmar was one of the stops on his South East Asian travels.

AND SO IT BEGINS

Monday, June 2, 2014

I wake up early. Like 5:30 a.m. It is my first day of work and I am not sure what to expect. I confess that I haven't been sleeping that well. I suppose my body has not quite adjusted to this time zone. I had already carefully selected my outfit on Sunday evening before going out to dinner with Adam. I settled on a royal blue pencil skirt with a white buttoned-up top and my nude heels. Adam and I are to leave at 7:50 a.m. to head to the office and it is 6:30 a.m. now as I have spent one hour writing. I shower, dress and go down to breakfast.

I am feeling a bit overwhelmed today. Perhaps it is the lack of sleep. Perhaps the reality is now hitting me that this will be my life for the next few months. Today is the first day I cried in the shower, but it is probably all the stress associated with the transition and the pent-up emotion of being in a new place. It is nice here so far, but I don't know if I want to stay. I search the room at breakfast for Khing, but I don't see him. I am about to ask one of the other servers for him when he appears. I am happy to see his familiar face. He makes my mornings. Now to the lobby to meet Adam.

* * *

We have just arrived at the office. I am to be managing a team of local lawyers here in Myanmar. While I will be managing a total of twenty-eight local advisors, only ten (eight males and two females) actually sit in the Yangon office with me which we classify as Myanmar South. The other eighteen are scattered in Myanmar North in various other regions such as Mandalay. They are all Burmese.

I notice that the guys wear white shirts and longyis to work and the ladies wear elegant traditional dress. They speak Burmese and I have no idea what they are saying. Thank God for the translator Than Tun whose English is pretty good. He explained to me that he previously worked as a tour guide but was hired as a translator by the company. He tells me he learnt his English from watching American movies and I smile. We have an open plan seating set-up in the Legal Department. Adam's desk is to my right, Than Tun sits directly in front of me and Htun Htun, the senior lawyer, sits to my left. Over the coming days I will try to learn the names of all my team members. I am excited about this unique challenge. They have all placed name tags on their desks to help me learn their names and I am happy as I think about how thoughtful they are.

Later in the day I finally see a familiar face. Anton, a colleague who had previously worked with me in the Caribbean, is here in the Yangon office. He heard from another colleague that I had arrived and he came over to my desk to say hello. It is a relief to see someone I actually know.

I am introduced to the company's CFO, Aaron, who is from the UK and who says he has been to Barbados five times and normally stays in Holetown in the parish of St. James and sometimes in St. Peter. I later learn that his partner is here in Yangon with him and that they are staying near the golf course. It seems a bit far out from the office to me. I just couldn't imagine that commute in the mornings, but that doesn't appear to bother him. He seems pleasant enough and again he welcomes me to the team warmly. I also meet the CEO, Murray. He is very likeable and thinks I have just arrived from Jamaica. I smile and correct him. He, too, has been to Barbados and tells me he stayed at the Royal Pavilion.

After all the introductions to the key people and to the various departments and a tour of the office, I spend the morning finding out exactly what each person on the team is responsible for. I also receive my local SIM and I have introductory calls with the other legal advisors who are not based in the Yangon office with me. Before I know it, it is midday.

The Burmese lawyers all clear out at noon for lunch with the exception of one young lady, Mima. She is a lovely girl with a face like a full moon and long dark hair to her behind. She comes to my desk and asks me how I am doing. She also asks me how old I am and when I tell her she exclaims that I am young. I wonder how old she thought I was. She is 34, or is it 24? I am not sure. Adam has disappeared into the boardroom for some peace and quiet and I don't blame him. The office is a bit chaotic. This is not unlike any of the other offices; everyone is scurrying around and acting busy.

My first task was to amend an undertaking. As the employees are not native English speakers it is a bit of a challenge, so I had to amend the undertaking significantly. The document had us making all kinds of undertakings for the health issues of the neighbours. These are not undertakings we can make. My next task will be reviewing a bilateral agreement which apparently was sent out without the Legal Department's prior review. I see two of the other expats, Noah and Evan, whom I met on Saturday. When I have a moment, I copy the names from the name tags on my team's desk to my notepad. I will learn their names and which faces go with which names by the end of the week.

I have lunch with Adam at a French bakery which is not too far from the office. It is a nice little spot. A diamond in the rough that is Yangon.

The food is fresh, and the place is clean. I wonder about the French being in Yangon and later learn that France is the 12th largest investor in Myanmar. Yangon is a little run down and dirty, but it also has this charm that draws you in. While collecting our lunch, Adam introduces me to Marcus from Jamaica. Marcus has caramel-coloured skin and curly hair which he wears a bit wild and has a face that reminds me of Detective Tubbs from *Miami Vice*. He has an infectious smile and I can see why all the ladies love him, as Adam told me. Marcus explains that he has finished up his stint in Yangon and is to return his laptop today. As we sit at our table, Adam tells me that Marcus is keen to stay in Myanmar and wants to open an F&B establishment. I suppose life is cheaper and somewhat easier here than in Jamaica. As we are eating our lunch, Adam says that he is going to Nay Pyi Taw on Thursday to meet with the regulator to discuss infrastructure development. Nay Pyi Taw is the third largest city in Myanmar and is actually the new capital of Myanmar. I am told there is nothing to see there. The city has limited facilities but gets an uninterrupted supply of electricity — unusual in the country. It also boasts a 20-lane road. Adam and the others joke that it is "the road to nowhere".

Yangon, also called Rangoon, was the capital of Myanmar from 1948 to November 6, 2005 when the country's military rulers moved the seat of government 320km north to Nay Pyi Taw. Some of the locals tell me a story that the move may have been triggered by a warning from an astrologer about a foreign military attack. They call Nay Pyi Taw a ghost town. Yangon has more character. Because Adam is going to be away in Nay Pyi Taw, it means that I will have to make my lunch treks alone and I must get my bearings quickly. Yeah me.

Adam and I return from lunch just after 1 p.m. and I buckle down to do some more work. However, I am struggling to keep my eyes open and it is only 2:07 p.m. I guess it doesn't help that I have been awake since 3 a.m. I wish my body would hurry up and adjust to the time zone. I think lovingly of my place in Barbados and how easy it was for me to drive home at lunch time and take a power nap during the day. There will be none of that here. It is 3:34 a.m. in Barbados now. I am about three hours away from completing my work day and the folks in Barbados haven't even started theirs as yet. I am ready to go to sleep and staring at these legal documents written in Burmese does not help my extended exhaustion from the jet lag. I don't know how our in-house translator Than Tun manages to read and translate these documents. It looks like a series of circles and characters.

For a moment I am distracted by the hive of conversation happening among my teammates. It is interesting watching these exchanges in Burmese. They are quite animated, and the language is very expressive and tonal. I just watch them. I can tell by the tone of their voices and their body language that something is not right. From their bits and pieces of English words, I gather that there seems to be a problem with our certificate of incorporation; it is expiring in the next month. As I am watching the team's exchanges, Than Tun, the translator, reminds me that Htun Htun will soon make a presentation to me on Burmese land law. At that moment, I gather my laptop and notebook and Than Tun accompanies me to the boardroom where Htun Htun is waiting.

* * *

Htun Htun was very good with his presentation. He helped me understand the different types of classifications of land in Myanmar a lot better. And there are so many different classifications! There are farmland/agricultural land, permit land, grant land, freehold land, village land/town land, religious land, forest land, vacant land/fallow land and virgin land. There is also military land and squatter land.

The Foreign Investment Law passed on November 2, 2012 and Foreign Investment Rules published in January 2013 state that the Myanmar Foreign Investment Commission may, for the purposes of promoting investment, allow investment to be made on any type of land that is legally registered in the name of the person who is entitled to lease the land, in accordance with the existing laws and with the prior approval of government. This section has an impact on site acquisition as we will only be able to lease certain types of lands to erect telecommunications infrastructure.

He started the presentation just after 3 p.m. and finished around 5:30 p.m. It is now 6:02 p.m. and I am ready to leave for the day, but I see that Adam is still busy making calls. I am beginning to understand slowly what everyone means when they say the Burmese people are lovely. They truly are. Everyone today was so helpful and wanted to make sure I am settling in okay. I am pleased that I have had a really good first day in the office, but I am ready for a nap.

The office is located in a grungy-looking building/shopping complex, but inside the actual office is quite clean. I wait for a few more moments, but Adam doesn't seem to be any closer to finishing so I take the taxi back to the hotel alone. I suppose Adam is preparing me for those times when he is not around. I stand by the side of the road and manage to flag down a taxi and the taxi driver charges me K3,000 which is US$3. It was only after I was getting ready to leave Myanmar that I learnt from my Burmese colleagues that the taxi drivers were charging me "tourist prices" all along. Once back at the hotel I retreat to my room and crash. Today was a full day and it was only my first day at the office. When I wake up, I suddenly get a craving for some KFC, which is crazy because I do not even like KFC and there are no KFC restaurants in Yangon. I decide that the craving must be my body's response to being away from home and in an unfamiliar place. Or maybe it is ready for something to eat since my last meal was a while ago. As I think about what should be my next meal, I think about the street food in Myanmar and an earlier conversation I had with Adam. It is still unthinkable to me that Adam would want to eat street food. I have no desire for it. On nearly every corner something is boiling, steaming or sizzling. The smell and faces of a street change about every hour, so don't use a street food vendor as a landmark to help you find your bearings or you will literally find yourself lost. These are nomadic vendors who often move to different streets to set up their food stalls. Some street food vendors just have a cart with a portable stove and ingredients to cook their treats, while others have more elaborate setups with small tents and low plastic tables and chairs for their customers and a large pot or two for whatever is cooking. Deep-fried breadsticks (imagine a donut but not exactly circular), fried noodles, fried rice, samosa salad, rice cakes (think pancakes), crepes, fried insects, sauces and soups are served in clear plastic bags and chicken (sometimes hanging from a hook in the stall) are all on offer. My doctor warned me off "eating the people's street food" before I left Barbados. His exact words were, "Leave the people's street food alone." He went on to explain that consuming street food can lead to food poisoning, especially if your immune system has not built up immunity to the various types of bacteria on offer. I am wary of it because food hygiene standards do not seem high on their list of priorities. Hot fried items are placed in plastic bags, food is left uncovered for extended periods of time and unwashed plastic bowls and plates are seen around the street food stalls. I finally ring down and ask room service to bring me some spaghetti aglio e olio. That is plainish and safe and seems like a good choice. After eating it is 12 a.m., so I try to go to bed.

DAY 2 AT THE OFFICE

Tuesday, June 3, 2014

I am slowly learning the names of the members of my team. It feels strange to be managing a group of lawyers who do not speak English. I am not sure if they are talking about me, laughing with me or laughing at me. I don't mind, but it is strange. I imagine that they are working, but I don't know. They all look busy. I want them to try and speak more English, but I don't know if this is right. I justify it in my mind that speaking more English will help them in the long run. Still, I am conflicted because I feel like the colonisers who came and imposed their language on the indigenous people.

Perhaps I should try to learn their language. The CEO just passed by our department. I wonder what his story is. Why is he here? I read online that Myanmar used to be considered a hardship posting. I wonder if he chose this posting or was it mandatory? Did his family accompany him? How long has he been here? An email pops up and interrupts my thoughts. A colleague in the Permitting Department drafted a document and sent it out without legal approval. She may be a problem. I have to go and have a meeting with her shortly.

Later in the day while I am chatting with Adam about how our respective days are going, he says that I can knock off early and I decide to take him up on the suggestion. My body continues to refuse to comply with the time difference and is still struggling to complete the day in the office once lunch time has passed. I pack up my things as fast as I can without seeming too excited and exit stage left. I am a firm believer that you don't need to be in the office or be chained to your desk to get your work done. I get that at times you need to be physically there, but I am sure that the lawyers whom I am managing are glad to see me leave early sometimes.

Once again, I take a taxi alone and I am deposited at my hotel. I am getting the hang of this thing, I think. I shower to wash off the grunge of Yangon and feel happy that I took the opportunity to leave early as it is starting to rain. There is something about a downpour that causes your bed to call out to you and I hastily respond by crawling into it and promptly falling asleep.

I am awakened from my sleep by the sound of my phone ringing. Still groggy, I reach for it on my night stand and answer. It is Adam reminding me that Ava, who works in the Human Resources Department, is taking us out to this new place called The Lab. I had totally forgotten about this. I am between minds on whether to stay in bed and make up some excuse as to why I can't make it. However, I decide to take the opportunity to go out and experience another side of life in Yangon. Plus, I wasn't in the mood to eat hotel food again. I have about two main items on the menu that I alternate between — the spaghetti aglio e olio or the vegetable fried rice with no egg, as I am allergic to eggs. They seem to put eggs in almost everything here. Adam texts me the address and I quickly jump out of my bed and get ready. I pull on my pencil jeans and a black top and slip my feet into my black pumps. I go down to the front desk, show them the address on my phone and tell them I need a taxi to that address and one is summoned for me.

It is dark now as I sit in the backseat of the taxi on my way to meet Adam, Ava and the others, but I am not scared. I am amazed at how safe I feel in this place. I feel safer here than in New York or even my own home country which is known for its low crime rate. I notice my taxi driver seems to be hesitant about which turns to make and he explains that he cannot find the location. I call Adam and he puts the waiter on to talk to the taxi driver. The taxi driver turns around and I spot a sign that says "The Lab". I pay him and hop out. I see Adam, Ava and Noah sitting at a table near the middle of the dimly lit room and they wave me over. The Lab is a new tapas restaurant with high tables, high chairs and exposed brick walls. Nearly every table is full because it is also two-for-one on sangria night. The atmosphere is lively and I am grateful for the company. Noah is hilarious. He was cracking jokes on various things the entire night. They ask me what was my initial reaction to Yangon. I say it has lots of potential and they agree. Yangon could look a lot different in a few years. Noah says he is suffering from cabin fever and I can understand how that can happen in a place like Yangon, but I am not anywhere near there yet.

When I return to my hotel room and reflect on my evening at The Lab and replay the night's conversation in my head, I notice there is one common thread running among us — we all are trying to find something in this place that seems to be at times forgotten by others. I change my WhatsApp profile picture to the day I was called to the bar. It serves as a reminder to me that I have overcome challenges before and reminds me that I can again. I get ready for bed and remember I haven't seen Khing today. I wonder if today is one of his days off. I must remember to ask him how to spell his name to ensure I am spelling it correctly.

MIMA

Wednesday, June 4, 2014

It is only my third day in the office and I notice that there seems to be the usual office politics. I guess that is inevitable as long as people are involved. Adam tells me there are issues with people expensing meals and taking vacations. It seems like he always has his ear to the ground of the happenings. There will always be people who will try to take advantage of the situation.

I have an offsite meeting at the coffee shop downstairs with Elliot and Su from the Government Relations Department and Adam. Su is Burmese and in her early 30s, but she is not wearing traditional dress like the other females in the office. Like most Burmese, she has hair all the way down to the middle of her back. She is quite elegant. I could see one of the expat men snapping her up. Elliot looks the activist part with long blonde hair. I learn that he is in Yangon with his wife Bea. He swears and expresses his disdain for "f***ing expats". I laugh to myself at the irony of it, since he is also an expat.

After the meeting, Padhraic, another colleague, joins us for lunch. Padhraic and I have the fact that we have both worked in the Eastern Caribbean in common, and we dominate the conversation for a while with tales of LIAT. He shares his experience and says he has no desire to live in the Caribbean again. Something must have happened, but I don't pry. Not many people I have met wouldn't like to live in the Caribbean again. I remember once I had an interview for a role in Brussels and the interviewer was very concerned that I would want to give up living in the Caribbean for Brussels. Padhraic was based in the South Pacific and confirms many of the stories we heard. He used to be picked up every morning for work by security. He says he is happier in Yangon, especially since he has more freedom here, and wants to stay as long as he can. I cannot relate, but I am new and must give the place time.

Later, as I sit at my desk typing away, I get a message:

Hi Nadia,

How are you? Are you tired or have a fever? If you need medicine, I take for you.
If you need my help, I help you anytime....!
09423710494
This is my phone number.
I always welcome you.........

Best regards,
Mima

I am heartened by the message. She comes over to my desk and tells me that she is from the Mon State, which is located on the western coast of South East Myanmar but lives in Yangon with her friends because of work. She comes across as a nice and genuinely good person and is always willing to help. I have misplaced my Face a Face US$700 designer glasses to help with my astigmatism. I swear I see one of the Burmese men wearing them and I laugh to myself. I definitely feel like I am in a twilight zone. I want someone to wake me up from this dream. I keep wondering if maybe I went mad and am really lying in a hospital bed in Barbados. I can only think that I must be crazy when I see men walking around wearing skirts and I can't understand a word they are saying. Mima asks me for my Skype ID and I happily oblige. I also give her a sweet. I can see we may become friends.

It is now 3:33 p.m. and, like clockwork, I am starting to wane. This is largely because my body has still not adjusted to the time zone and the fact that some monks who live next to the hotel start drumming at 4 a.m. does not help. I later learn that the drumming is to wake them up to pray. Noah and Adam think that they drum at four in the morning because they are always farting around during the day and therefore are not tired like regular people at 4 a.m. My lack of focus is compounded by the incessant drilling from renovations being done in the building which houses our office. How am I supposed to do any work or even concentrate when the drilling is so loud that it sounds like it is in the next room?

The entire office is concerned about one of our lawyers, Win Tin, who is missing from the office. We later find out from U Nu who was able to reach Win Tin's wife that he had an accident and has to get a tetanus shot. He was wearing slippers outside his house and accidentally stepped on a nail.

I have to go and speak to the CFO about resolutions. Landowners changing their minds and the incessant drilling are getting to me. I bring it to Adam's attention that a landowner no longer wants to proceed because she has built a house on the land she was going to lease us. I am told we will pay her US$500 to move the house. This project is for national development, after all. We must fulfil our contractual obligations and they should too.

I am tired of it all and just want to crawl into my bed and sleep. I am not feeling overwhelmed, thankfully. Just tired. Very tired. The lights flicker. The electricity going off is a common thing here. For once I am not disturbed about not having a window. I loved having a window in my office in Barbados where I could look outside and see when people were scooting off to the coffee shop. However, I do not want to see outside today as the rain is pouring. When it rains here in Yangon, the water levels rise quickly because of improper drainage and can sometimes reach up to knee level or higher. All manner of items can float along beside you. I have been on edge all day. I must cut down on the amount of coffee I have been drinking. Perhaps tomorrow will be better. It is now 4:27 p.m. I can hear the thunder rolling and the lightning is flashing.

I see Than Tun reading the newspaper which is printed in Burmese. It sounds like he has said, "I am done with this nonsense for the day" in Burmese and he cracks open some biscuits that Mima has given to the team and puts down the newspaper. It seems as though he is also in a foul mood today. I am told that the Burmese staff like going to movies. I cannot blame them; I would want to escape that way too.

Htun Htun makes me smile. I watch him closely and I can see his sense of satisfaction every time he sends an email in English and I am very proud of him. I decide that I am going to make an effort to learn Burmese and help him to improve his English. It is 5:33 p.m. and Adam has disappeared. I want to go home...well, to the hotel. I have accepted that it is my home for now. I catch Anton at the corner of my eye when I am leaving, but I make no eye contact because I don't feel like chatting. I am tired and I want to go home. It is still raining outside so I open my umbrella. I do not want to do anything tonight. I make it to the hotel and take my usual shower and weep at the thought of the distance I am away from home in case anything should happen to me. I check the clocks to see the time in Barbados. It is early morning hours there so no one will be awake. I suppose I will stop doing this crying thing eventually.

Crying is my release. I suppose no one sent me here and I was advised to think long and hard about my decision before I made it. I want to ask someone if I am really here. This all seems strangely familiar like I dreamt this before, or I was already here.

THE FRENCH BAKERY
IS THE SPOT

Thursday, June 5, 2014

I feel a bit better today. Once I pass certain points in the day, I am fine. At breakfast Khing briefly stops at my table and asks if I have started working and I tell him yes and that I am learning a lot, but then I have to dash off and get my taxi.

Lately, there has been a shady-looking Asian I have been noticing at breakfast every morning. He wears sunglasses indoors and is covered in tattoos. He looks like he is a member of the Japanese Yakuza and I wonder what brings him to Yangon. Maybe he is into human trafficking. I am careful to lock up my suitcase before leaving my hotel room now, but I am not even certain why. I don't remember bringing anything too valuable to Yangon.

I went out to lunch today alone for the first time. It was a lovely day. The sun was out, but it wasn't overly hot so I decided to eat lunch at the cute little French bakery which has become a sanctuary for me in the middle of my work days. I was so happy and content to be on my own. So much so that I felt like doing a little skip as I walked to the bakery. It is one of the few places I have come across so far that doesn't serve

Asian food which suits me quite fine because I was getting tired of it and need some variety. As I am about to place my order, I see Marcus there and, once I collect my order, I walk over to say hello before I head back to the office.

The French bakery is out of baguettes, so I have the chicken salad. It cost me K4,000, but it is worth every penny. I also have a latte which cost me K2,500. I head back to the office, bobbing and weaving through traffic. My confidence about being alone in Yangon is growing.

At the office, Mima continues to be a godsend and a great help to me. She shows me which Wi-Fi network to connect to if I am going to use Gmail or Facebook. I wonder if management knows about this, although I doubt it very much. Today was Saoirse's goodbye celebration in the boardroom. Saiorse was part of the C-suite. I really didn't have a chance to work with her, but the staff here seems to love her. She is very emotional as colleagues shower her with gifts and speeches. I remember that episode of *The Good Wife* where Will is shot and the intern who barely knows him for three weeks is fired for crying. I dare not cry.

L'OPERA

Friday, June 6, 2014

On the ride to work Adam explains to me why The Strand was so empty on Sunday night when we went. I do not hear him as I am busy looking out the window and making a mental note of the buildings we pass. The taxi drivers do not take the same route each morning in an attempt to beat the traffic and this morning this particular driver has taken a "shortcut" that I haven't seen before.

As soon as I arrive at the office the receptionist pulls me aside and hands me my Face a Face glasses which I had misplaced earlier. She said she found them in the boardroom. I am ecstatic that I have them back and in perfect condition. Maybe the Burmese man whom I thought I had seen wearing them forgot them there. I thought I had lost them for good. I couldn't for the life of me figure out where they could have gone. I had asked at the hotel and maybe thought I had lost them permanently in a taxi. I thank the receptionist profusely and give her my Oreo cookies as a token of appreciation.

There is an extra pep in my step now that I have been reunited with my glasses and I make my way to my desk to begin the day's tasks. The documents in front of me are "interesting" to read. There is an issue and someone needs to go to speak to the village chief. I am told this is code for when the village chiefs want money to pass under the table. No one is particularly bothered by this. Htun Htun shows me where the smokers' section outside the rooftop is. I have not taken back up smoking yet, even though I have considered it. The cigarettes are very cheap here, about K500, which roughly works out to about 50 US cents.

I have lunch with Adam and Noah at an interesting place. It is off the usual path and a very local place. There are mostly locals there and only one more table with people dressed in work attire like us. There are no airs and graces about this place. Noah led the way as we crisscrossed through a set of alleyways and across an abandoned parking lot just to get there. If I had to do the reverse alone I would be utterly lost. The entrance is through a "doorway" that makes you feel like you are sitting outside. I don't know the name of it, but it is somewhere that Noah discovered. He is happy to discover new places and try new things. I suppose he is the kind of person you want around. During lunch, he and Adam chat about the rugby game that is showing on Saturday. I am not into rugby. I hear them say that the All Blacks will be playing and they make plans to go and see it. This is, of course, after we finish work. Apparently, some sort of edict went out that expats are expected to work on Saturdays from 10 a.m. to 2 p.m. The benches at this place Noah has brought us to reminds me of Kermitt's, a rustic rum shop on the south coast of Barbados. The menu is in Burmese but thankfully it has pictures so I point to what I would like. I order the tamarind juice but forget to tell them not to include any ice. I hope the water they used to make the drink and the ice are not contaminated. I order the chicken satay which seems like the safest thing on the menu. I am making a conscious effort to play it safe since it is my first foray into eating meat in Yangon. Noah has the grilled fish and Adam has a noodle meal. Note to self: never order the noodles. I cannot use chopsticks and they do not have forks in these local places. It would be a disaster. Noah's fish is massive with the head on and everything. I wish I had remembered my phone so I could take a picture of it. He says we are welcome to try it, but I dare not try it. I am not sure which river they caught the fish from and I can't imagine getting sick in a foreign country.

On the way back to the office we meet our colleague Alejandro, accompanied by his wife and daughter, in the lobby of the building. It appears he has just finished his lunch as well and is about to say goodbye to them. He is from Ecuador (or somewhere in South America/Central America), I think. His daughter is adorable, but she is tired and cranky and doesn't want to talk and is holding on to her father's neck for dear life. I suppose having your family close by helps with the transition. I have no one close by.

Meanwhile, back at the office, an email pops up from Than Tun. He sends back a translation of a one-page lease in Burmese. I cannot verify a word it says and hope he has translated it correctly and that he has not mixed up the obligations of lessor and lessee.

Even if I cannot read it, I must be able to understand what they are saying at least. I am even more resolved to learn the language. Htun Htun is a star. He suggests we add an indemnity clause to the one-pager, and I am pleased that he is taking the initiative and making suggestions instead of me having to pry everything out of him with my questions as I have had to do for the past few days. I thank him in Burmese and he cheekily says, "Let's see if the owner accepts." I laugh. I have asked Than Tun to teach me the language and he has agreed. I am excited to get started. The electricity goes off.

The team teaches me a few Burmese phrases — 'hello' and 'thank you' — to pass the time as the electricity has gone off. They are generally happy that I am making an effort to communicate with them in their language. Half an hour later the electricity is still off. My laptop still has three hours of battery life to go. That three hours would put me at 5:32 p.m. I am trying to decide if I should return to the hotel and work from there. The reality is, the electricity could possibly be off at the hotel, too, but at least there is a generator there. U Nu fills the silence with his singing. I ask Win Tin how his foot is feeling now and he shows me his lost toenail. It looks ghastly, but he says it is okay. I can tell you, no one I know would have entered the office with their toe in such a state. But he is here, and I am grateful for his attendance.

The Legal Department is directly across from the lunchroom and I see a Burmese boy staring at me. When I look in his direction he looks down at the floor. I wonder what is wrong. I am happy for them that they at least have jobs. Mima makes me some coffee and brings me some Pucci special cake. It is tasty and not as sweet as I thought it would have been. Even though I am not hungry I sip my coffee and nibble at the cake so as not to offend. She is so kind. They are always bringing me food here. The same way they bring food to Buddha.

When I have finished my cake and coffee Htun Htun passes me a Post-it Note with his number written on it. I ask him what he normally does on the weekends and he tells me that he goes to the church close to his house. Then he asks me which church I go to. I tell him in Barbados I go to the Anglican church sometimes. In reality, I haven't been to church in a long time. I did go to Skye's (my friend Juann's daughter's) christening recently, but I am not sure that counts, and that was a Moravian church. I see Htun Htun looking at his watch and I decide not to insist that he stay and finish the assignment I gave to him. I tell him he can finish it on Monday and he is happy. He says he has a friend who goes to the Anglican church and he will introduce him to me next week so I can go. I am impressed. Who would have thought I would be going to church in Myanmar? I tell him I will come to work in the morning then go to the market later. He asks me what time I am going to the market and I tell him probably after 2 p.m. Htun Htun is one of the nicest people I have ever met.

Than Tun, who sits directly in front of me, overhears the conversation between Htun Htun and me about the weekend and says he is going to his mother-in-law's house for the weekend. I learn that Than Tun's birthday is in January and he is married and has two brothers. He and his wife live at his father's house and they are going to his mother-in-law's house this weekend so that his wife can visit her mother. Adam joins in the conversation and says he was born in December.

Also overhearing the conversation and gathering that I had no plans for the weekend, Adam later sends me a text and asks if I am up for dinner. Of course I am. Noah says he is tired so he won't join us. I can't blame him. I really wouldn't want to join us either — it can be a bit monotonous working and "playing" with colleagues all the time and we are not exactly the life of the party either. Noah parties really hard and is probably justifiably tired. A taxi is summoned for us and the hotel staff explain to the taxi driver in Burmese that we are going to L'Opera, an Italian restaurant. We drive around and the taxi driver has to ask about six people how to get there. It is hilarious and I feel for the poor taxi driver. Because I do not yet fully understand the language, I swear one man tells him, "Carry them down the road and put them out, man." The taxi driver takes us to Le Planteur, the French restaurant. We do not want to go there. He drives again and asks someone else. I am in fits of laughter in the backseat of the taxi. When we get there, I pay him more than the fare he quoted us for the journey. It is the best laugh I have had since being in Yangon.

We have dinner at L'Opera. It is a fine dining restaurant in a colonial-type building surrounded by well-manicured gardens on Inya Lake. The warm lighting in the garden makes it look magical. Our host offered us the choice of indoor or outdoor seating and we decide to sit inside as we were worried about the mosquitoes in the garden. The place is lovely and sitting in the restaurant I could be anywhere in the world — Barbados, Italy, New York — except our entire wait staff looks Asian. To start, I have the caprese con mozzarella di bufala, which is slices of buffalo mozzarella cheese with tomato and homemade pesto, and for my main I have lasagna ai funghi, which is layers of baked pasta with tomato and béchamel sauce and mushrooms. The food is divine.

I comment to Adam that, sitting in this place, it is easy to forget we are in Yangon. The place is full of mostly white expats having dinner. Apart from Marcus and Badrick who work with us and another guy I saw at the Pagoda, there are very few black people here. I long to see another black woman like myself to ask her how she manages with her hair here. I have to wash mine tomorrow and I am wearing a weave for the first time as suggested by my hairdresser. She suggested this protective style as she was worried about my own hair breaking, since her confidence in me being able to find a hairdresser who could care for my hair type was low.

The expat women in the office haven't warmed up to me yet so I don't have much choice at the moment in terms of female contact. It is either them, Mima or Su. Dinner is pleasant enough; Adam and I have a lot in common in terms of the movies we like. We talk about the *Godfather* movies and *Fight Club*. I tell him about the books I have read and he speaks about his upbringing in New Zealand. There were four of them in all and his parents simply didn't have the time. He was raised Pentecostal, so he makes jokes about the flags and clapping and tambourines. I understand since I attended a Nazarene church as a child where there was lots of clapping and tambourines, but no flags. He, however, is the first white person I have met so far who was raised Pentecostal. The ones I had met were mostly raised Catholic or Anglican where there is no clapping or tambourines. At L'Opera they actually bring the dessert out for you to choose. How could you resist seeing those treats in living colour? I choose one that looks absolutely delicious, with chocolate, of course, and Adam and I share it. We split the bill and then summon a taxi back home to the hotel.

When we get to the hotel, we part ways. Adam heads to have a beer with the remainder of the expats who are staying there, minus Noah. The South African is there. He wears a bumbag around his waist and has an air of arrogance, especially as he uses terms like "you people". There are two other South Africans as well who are more palatable. I do not have the energy or the head space to deal with him. Truth be told, I am a little tired and I may only scream at him. This is not South Africa. I am weary of him. He complains about per diem. I do not get a good vibe or good energy from him and our exchange earlier in the day made it even worse.

In the office earlier today after 5 p.m. when everyone was trying to complete their tasks for the day to go home, he waltzed up to where we were sitting and asked for a lawyer to complete a task that would take about six hours' drive to get to, for something that was not even a legal issue. This would have meant that the individual who needed to go would be sacrificing his or her Saturday. My lawyers have lives and families too and it was a rubbish request. You need to give your colleagues proper notice. Then he commented to Adam, "Oh, she can go", looking in my direction. I gave him such a look. Who is "she"? Furthermore, I do not speak Burmese, so how could I have gone on that mission? I politely told him it is not a legal issue so we wouldn't be able to help him, then I packed up my things and left for the hotel.

MY WAITER KHING

Saturday, June 7, 2014

I have breakfast a little later than normal this morning and Khing is his usual chatty self as he serves me. He shows me pictures of his wife and daughter. His daughter is 2 1/2 years old and she is gorgeous. He says he will invite me to lunch or dinner on one of his days off.

It is Saturday and I take the advantage of returning to my room to sleep after breakfast. When I wake up it is nearly midday and I feel so rested. I needed those extra hours of sleep to make up for the hard time I have been having during weekday mornings. It is my first full Saturday in Yangon, so I don't have to go into the office since I am still a bit jet lagged. I tell myself I cannot sleep all day, so I get dressed to go to the Bogyoke Aung San Market. I try to change US$100 to kyats in case I want to buy anything, even though I doubt there will be anything I want to purchase there. However, the girl at the front desk lets me know they do not accept US bills that have been folded. I have to go back upstairs and look for money that hasn't been folded. This is tiring.

Once I get my currency changed a taxi is summoned for me. There is lots of traffic. The driver says that it is normally about 15 minutes, but it is a lot longer today because of the traffic. Since they opened up the country too many vehicles have been imported and the roads are not equipped for them. Eventually the taxi driver announces we are here, and I am deposited on the sidewalk. Bogyoke Aung San Market is a huge market bazaar located in the Pabedan Township. The office and my hotel are in the Bahan Township. Townships are the subdivisions within the seventy-six districts in Myanmar. The Pabedan and Bahan Townships are about 10 minutes away from each other, but it takes 40 minutes to get there because there is so much traffic on the road. I am starting to get a sense of where places are. The Bogyoke Aung San Market reminds me of Cheapside Market in Barbados but on a much grander scale. I walk around and take in the sights and smells of the market. There are tourists there. A huge black Range Rover drives down one of the narrow cobblestone streets. I wonder what it is doing down there since it looks so out of place. The market has a huge number of shops selling clothes, antiques, jade jewellery and food stuff. A Burmese boy offers me some tea, but I decline. I buy a few things, mostly souvenirs.

When it starts to rain, I take my leave of the market and pay a taxi driver K4,000 to take me back to the hotel. I know I am being overcharged, but I don't really care. He speaks to his colleague in Burmese and it sounds like he says, "She didn't even haggle." I get back and housekeeping is cleaning my room, so I sit in the lobby and talk to Khing. He asks me where I went to and I show him my pics. He asks if no one took my picture at the market and when I tell him no, he takes a photo of me in the hotel lobby and I take one of him. He is such a sweetheart. I value our exchanges and I appreciate his concern for me. He says I should give the street food time since my stomach probably won't be able to take it. I do not tell him that I have no intention of trying the street food at all. I am even sceptical of the roadside BBQs in Barbados.

I have lunch at the hotel and I meet Lynette from Singapore. We are drawn together by our mutual love for Longchamp bags. She has a large red one and I am toting my off-white one today. I explain what I am doing in Myanmar and she tells me that she works for an international children's charity and she shares her story with me. Lynette is here teaching Communications to Myanmar businesses. I think what she is doing is admirable. Teaching is admirable and teaching adults in a foreign country where English is not their native language deserves a medal. She is leaving for Singapore shortly, but she gives me her card. I finish my lunch and head back up to find my room clean and the room attendant gone. I upload the pictures to my computer and then take a nap at 3 p.m.

When I wake up it is 5 p.m. I wash my hair which doesn't turn out to be as bad as I had thought. I imagined it would have been a mass of knots and tangles and the threads the weave is sewn in with would have come undone, but everything is still intact. I am so pleased with how my hair has turned out that I want to go out. I step outside and the footmen are ready to summon a taxi for me, but I tell them that I will walk instead. I head in the direction of a restaurant called the Vietnam Kitchen just as outside is starting to get dark. There are no streetlights and I feel like I should have walked with my flashing light that I used for running in Barbados. There are men on the road and I am conscious of their eyes following me as I make my way down the street. I wonder if it is because they view me as a tourist or because women do not generally walk around alone here. However, I do not feel afraid at all, a testament that my confidence is growing and I am moving outside of my comfort zone. I really wouldn't walk about in my own home country at night alone. I live about five minutes away from the yoga studio in Barbados and still I do not walk there at night. Being somewhere new will force you to reflect and analyse yourself. I eat my meal, which is a Vietnamese dish of fried rice and saltfish, and walk back to the hotel. I hit the sack at 10:27 p.m. This was my second Saturday night in Myanmar, although I couldn't really count the first as I had only arrived that Saturday.

A WALK TO KANDAWGYI PARK
AND THE SOUTH AFRICAN

Sunday, June 8, 2014

I wake up and I feel rested. It is probably the best rest I have had since being in Yangon. I shower and go down to breakfast around 9:15 a.m. with ample time to have breakfast before they stop serving at 10:00 a.m. The fried vermicelli is growing on me. It consists of fried rice noodles (rice sticks) which are made from flour, rice and water, and vegetables which include bean sprouts, and scallions and soy sauce for seasoning.

These types of selections are normal breakfast food here. I would never have eaten this or eaten so heavily in Barbados for breakfast. Breakfast was usually a cereal bar wolfed down as I drove to work or a bottle of Ensure.

I see a few new faces. There is a white couple and a white Rastafarian guy with tattoos, accompanied by his Asian girlfriend who is also tattooed. She is a brown Asian, not a light one, and I cannot tell where she is from. I am told that white skin is valued here. There is also another Asian family with kids. The mother is on her phone and looks stressed. I spot the South African getting his breakfast. He does not speak and neither do I.

As usual, Khing comes and talks to me. He asks what I did yesterday evening and I tell him about the Vietnam Kitchen. He reminds me about dinner at his home. I hope he doesn't live far away. When he comes back to collect my plates after I am finished, he asks if I do not like the tempura because I left most of it back on my plate. It is not that I don't like it, I explain, I just find that it is greasy. I don't think my stomach can take the grease. I have to admit, though, that since I have been eating the yogurt at breakfast my stomach has been feeling better. Khing says with a sly smirk that gradually I will be able to stomach most things. The statement is not lost on me and I think he may be right.

I return to my hotel room and I am happy I will have a few moments to write. Kim who works in finance in the Barbados office is online so I chat with her briefly. I would normally just sign out of Microsoft Lync, but I stay on today and tell her about my experience so far. She ends the conversation by saying, "Take care of yourself." I smile. There is only me to take care of me here.

I head out to Kandawgyi Park which Adam told me about when I first came. I am finally getting to go and the sun is already beating down. I am deliberately wearing a tube top because it is so hot and I open my umbrella to shield myself from the sun like the Burmese women do. I would previously only have opened my umbrella for the rain. As I make my way to the park, there are Burmese boys shouting at me, exclaiming how beautiful I am and asking me where I am going. I am amused. Their behaviour reminds me of the men in the Caribbean and I realise that some things remain the same, even when you are ten thousand miles away from home. This is the first time this has happened here, though. Boys will be boys. It is probably that they are young. Men here tend to be more respectful. The park, which is surrounded by a huge lake, is full of people — mostly young couples — when I arrive. I am not surprised as I was told that most of the young people come to the park to court. I am charged K2,000 to enter. I walk around and a guy who is also a tourist takes my picture for me with my camera. He then asks me to return the favour and I happily oblige. The park is lovely and I am grateful there is somewhere like this to escape to in the city. The weather, though, is very hot and humid, so I stand in the shade of a tree and take in the atmosphere of young people walking hand in hand, young couples playing with their children and tourists snapping pictures of the place and of each other. When I have had enough of the park, I walk back to the hotel. I am dripping wet by now despite my decision to wear a tube top.

I come back from the park and do not head immediately to my room. I am enjoying being out of the confines of the four walls of my room and I am enjoying the cool air in the lobby. I try to figure out what to do for lunch since it is getting close to 2 p.m. The electricity goes off briefly and the South African sees me sitting in the lobby as he is about to go into the elevator. He comes over and starts a conversation. I wish he hadn't, but I try to be pleasant enough. He tells me about his home base in Pretoria, his farm and his wife. His brother is running the farm for him now that he is over here in Yangon. He plans to buy another farm when he returns to South Africa. He also has other properties there which he plans to sell when he returns because the world economy is picking up so people are buying again. He thinks the government they have now is shit. I want to ask him if he means the African National Congress (ANC), but I refrain because I know that the ANC is in power and Zuma is the president. As he speaks, I remember the prison guard in *Long Walk to Freedom* who tells Nelson Mandela that he did not need his job since his family has three farms. It is perhaps not by chance that this was the movie that I watched on the flight over here.

He tells me about his experience in other developing countries and getting a nice flat and a Land Cruiser to drive around. He has been to Mombasa, Kenya and some other places. He notes the locals here are friendly, but in other countries he has been in they are very hostile to whites. He hates Yangon, though, since he doesn't have a nice flat or a Land Cruiser. He is not interested in learning anything about the place. He just wants to get in and get out with as much money as possible.

After the South African leaves, I mentally make plans to visit South Africa one day. I am sure that it is a lovely place and I would enjoy the opportunity to explore it. I decide I am not going back outside in the heat and make my peace with hotel food. Keisha has insomnia so is awake and I chat with her for a bit before heading upstairs to write. It has been a good, quiet weekend.

FUN WEEK AT THE OFFICE

Monday, June 9, 2014

It is the start of a new week and my second one in Yangon. I feel rested and ready to tackle the world. It is interesting waking up in a foreign country every morning when you are not on holiday. I think the key now to feeling more rested is to go to bed early. I go down to breakfast and it is so crowded I cannot even get my usual seat. Khing is too busy to chat and that is okay with me. I am not inspired by any of the breakfast, so I eat the bare minimum and have some tea and then coffee.

I see Adam in the lobby as we both wait for a taxi to work and he tells me that he is not feeling well. He has a stomachache. I had been wondering why I had not seen him for the morning. He keeps experimenting with the food here, but he really needs to be more careful about what he eats. Poor fella. I tell him that tonic water and lime normally settles my stomach. We arrive at the office and are greeted by a mass of balloon decorations. Than Tun tells me it is Fun Week and so a variety of fun activities have been planned. The team wants to take pictures and I happily oblige. I save the team picture as the background picture for my laptop. This will keep me going throughout the day. I look across just in time to see Adam hustling to the bathroom once more. I feel so sorry for him. Stomachache is not a good thing.

We have a myriad of problems to tackle today. There is a landowner in Bago trying to extort money from us. As explained to me, during construction his fence was damaged and the company repaired it, but now he wants US$2,000 for damages. Damages for what, we do not know, because his fence has already been repaired. He wants the money by 12 p.m. today or he is going to sue us. I am of the opinion that we should not even be entertaining this. We have already repaired his fence. Call his bluff. Let him sue if he wants. We nevertheless need to be creative in our response as litigation and any negative publicity would be bad for the company. I draw up a release and Win Tin is going over there with it along with the site acquisition team to deal with this. He is taking US$500 with him. If the landowner insists on any more, the legal advisor is to tell him he needs management's approval and come back. I asked Than Tun what he thinks and he shares his opinion with me. He does not think we should give this landowner any more money.

Next on the list: We have entered into a lease with a local farmer; however, a big farming company sends an email to our company's chairman saying they are the owner of the property. Because the chairman is now involved this is priority and we have to urgently investigate who the rightful owner is.

As it is a fun day, we take a break from the work and I also have my caricature drawn. The artist gives me a long chin, but I think it is cute. There is a rumour that Ava tore up her caricature and Noah's caricature looks like The Wolverine. I think it is all good fun and a welcome change in the atmosphere at the office.

SETTLING IN

Tuesday, June 10, 2014

I am well into my second working week in Yangon and I feel as though I am still settling in. This morning on the ride up on the elevator Noah and Adam were teasing about my "bling shoes". I am wearing my favourite pair of Jorge Bischoff designer shoes today, a different pair from the ones I wore yesterday.

They say that I am dressed for New York while they are dressed for Yangon. I laugh at their jesting, but I can't help but feel a little guilty and out of place, and not for the first time I regret that I had not packed a little differently. However, I wasn't prepared to go shopping for new shoes to appease my conscience when I have pairs of perfectly good shoes already. Later in the morning I am sitting at my desk and I hear the ladies on my team practicing my name. This makes me smile. I am reminded that just as I am learning about them and their country they are also trying to get to know and understand more about me. I may still feel a little out of place, but Yangon and my colleagues are growing on me and I hope I am impacting them in some positive way as well.

I didn't write last night. Evan and Noah hailed me as I entered the hotel and invited me to have a drink. I told them I would be back. I went upstairs, put down my things and headed back down, not wanting to seem standoffish. Here there is pressure to socialise or you will find yourself isolated and alienated. We drank wine and Evan shared about his time in Mandalay, the second largest city in Myanmar. Yangon is the largest. We all talk about how each other's Monday went and about Yangon and shared our mutual dislike for the South African. They made jokes about how he takes his Tupperware container to breakfast and stocks it up.

Pat, another expat, was there and I was introduced to him yet again. Pat said he is 56, but he looks like 72 and is a lover of wine and women. He is from the UK but has been living in Uganda and is getting ready to finish up his stint here. He heard I am from Barbados and told me he used to work in Jamaica. Pat made small talk with us for a little while longer but decided he had had enough to drink for the night and took his leave. Evan's Burmese girlfriend joined us sometime after Pat departs. I do not know what her real name is, but they call her Kitty. She does look a bit like a cat. She was wearing a form-fitting red dress with heels instead of the traditional dress that is popular among Burmese women. There are rumours that she is a prostitute, but I am not sure.

I learned that she has a son with a man who was based in the South Pacific. I asked her how old her son is and she told me that I ask too many questions. She probably didn't want to say his age as I might have been able to place her age. Youth is valued in her supposed profession. I probably *was* asking her too many questions. After all, we had only just met. She did, however, disclose that she will be going to Bangkok soon to work, but she didn't say what kind of work.

Adam finally pulled up in the taxi and came to join us. He ordered the fried sea bass and I was amazed that he bravely continues his food adventure even after that bad stomachache. I am still sceptical about the fish. Evan and Noah made jokes that it was probably caught in the Yangon River not too far away. They are a riot and I enjoyed their company for the evening. It was a welcome change from staying in my room. We ordered another bottle of Red Mountain Estate wine (from the Shan State) and I ordered the chicken curry and jasmine rice as I was hungry by then. I am getting slightly more adventurous with my food choices but still maintaining some caution. That was the third item I have had on the menu, having exhausted the spaghetti and the vegetarian fried rice. By 10:30 p.m. I was ready to call it a night and Adam had already made his escape. I bade the guys and Kitty *au revoir* and took my leave. I headed straight for my bed, not even bothering to change or remove my bra. I slept soundly and didn't wake until I heard the monks next door drumming at 4 a.m.

* * *

As part of our Fun Week activities at work I am running the World Cup Sweepstakes. I cut out the flags of the 32 teams I find online and the list of teams. It is K2,000 to pick a team at random. Only the expats so far have chosen teams and not all of them either. I wonder if K2,000 is too much for the locals. I was told they are mad about football here but still not one local has come to me to choose a team yet. The new Pacific General Counsel and Group General Counsel are visiting next week and I have to prepare a presentation for them, but it is taking me way longer than I would like. I check the list to see what other activities are on for Fun Week and learn that there will be a birthday party later for all the staff celebrating their birthdays this month. I also check with Mima to see who will be updating her database while she is away on leave. She says that it is not a problem since she has the internet at home and can do it herself. I ask her if she is sure and she says it is fine. I do not understand because I know no one where I am from who will willingly agree to do work on their holiday, but I tell her okay. I will have a team meeting later to see who will update the database in her absence.

It is mid-morning and I try to push through the day, but I can't ignore the mild stomachache I am experiencing. I felt the curious sensation in my stomach just before I left for the office this morning, but I didn't think anything of it. It is probably the wine I drank last night or the curry chicken, I try to convince myself, because the possibility that I am getting sick in Yangon is terrifying.

We have a team meeting and I have made Ne Win and Khing Sa responsible for updating the databases while Mima is away. During the team meeting Adam announces that we will need a lawyer to work on Saturdays. This new requirement by management has been a controversial topic within the Legal Department and I am pleased when Htun Htun speaks out about it. Since it was not an initial term of employment, he raised the issue of whether overtime will be paid for the additional hours. He says that the team members have not been coming on Saturdays because overtime had not been discussed. We decide that they will take turns coming in. As their manager, I can't expect them to come in and I am not here, but I won't get any overtime for this.

As part of Fun Day today we also have to write positive mottos and put them on Post-it Notes. U Nu writes "I am the leader of my life" in English. I am happy for him that he has written this in English as he is the oldest on the team and mostly speaks Burmese. Just before lunch we have the motto competition and this is the motto that won the first prize: *Don't be afraid to give up the good to get the great.* The tiniest girl in the crowd is the one who wrote this. I do not even know her name and I have never seen her before now. She could easily be the Burmese version of me. It is one of those moments when I want someone to pinch me. I keep wondering if I am dreaming this up. I pinch myself, but I do not feel anything. This all seems strangely familiar. Am I dreaming, am I dreaming, am I dreaming? I probably should not have watched *Inception* before I left Barbados.

Even though I don't get a ton of work done today, I am able to have a conversation with Adam. I tell him that we shouldn't be bending over backwards and paying off these neighbours who have frivolous claims. If we pay one, we could just open the flood gates. Word gets around and it will never end. I am happy that I listened to Than Tun and we did not send Win Tin out there with money. They understand their culture better than I do.

I have a chat with Badrick who is Jamaican. I noticed he was headed to the lunchroom but he made a detour for my desk instead. Yesterday when he came over to my desk to ask if he could have some of the bottled water I was about to open to pour in his steaming hot coffee he told me the only things he likes hot are his ladies. Today he just came over to say hi and I take the opportunity to get him to select a team for the World Cup Sweepstakes. He tells me that he is happy to see someone else who looks like him. I smile because I can totally relate. I remember how overjoyed I was to see Marcus that day in the French bakery. I haven't seen him again since though. I wonder what has happened to him.

It is nearing six and Noah asks if I am ever going to leave work. Than Tun is still there and I feel guilty leaving when he still has a lot of work to do. I tell Noah I will leave in about ten minutes. I eventually leave and it is raining outside, but I manage to catch a cab quickly. Evan and Pat greet me outside the hotel. I don't see Noah, but I have no plans of going back down. I am happy to bond with my bed. As I make my way up to my room, I think about Than Tun and the fact that he has graciously agreed to teach me Burmese. I am looking forward to starting my language classes. He thinks we can do them after work. I am at least happy about that.

MATTHEW'S RETURN

Wednesday, June 11, 2014

Matthew, who works in one of the regional offices, is back from Nay Pyi Taw and we are going out later to celebrate his return. I haven't met Matthew yet, but I agree to go out. It beats spending the evening alone. I think that he is some kind of regional manager or something like that. I invariably know that this will involve drinking, but I am fine to go.

I leave the office around 6 p.m. and take a taxi back to the hotel. The taxi driver charges me K2,000 and I am surprised because it is normally K3,000. Maybe they see me so often that they have decided to give me a discount. I shower, pull on my favourite pair of jeans, a white T-shirt and my nude flats. It is raining so I suspect that we may not be leaving the hotel to go out. When I get downstairs, the guys are already drinking by the bar and I am introduced to Matthew. He is a stout fellow with brown hair. He is a Canadian, grew up in Toronto and has property in Halifax.

We drink and laugh and talk. They mention that they are anticipating the South Africans' arrival because they want to tell them off some more. Apparently, there was a very heated discussion the previous night when I was absent and Adam basically "read the riot act" to them. I would like to have seen that. They finally arrive and Matthew, who has not yet met the South Africans, gets to see what they are like. He agrees with the general opinion of them. We have had enough and decide to go out. I go to my room to get some cash, pin up my hair, put on some lipstick and get my heels. We pile into the taxi and head to the Sule Shangri-la Hotel. Evan is being very protective of me, like I am his daughter from Uganda that he told me about. The guys are getting louder and I can tell he is probably thinking it is only a matter of time before they try to chat me up, having had a few drinks. He is a softie deep down inside.

A SURPRISE CHAT

Thursday, June 12, 2014

Myanmar has three seasons: the cool, relatively dry northeast monsoon (late October to mid-February), the hot, dry inter-monsoon season (mid-February to mid-May), and the rainy southwest monsoon (mid-May to late October). A monsoon is a seasonal shift in the prevailing wind direction that brings a different type of weather.

The monsoon rains have finally arrived, slightly late this year, and we have barely made it to work in one piece. The roads are like huge lakes as it can rain heavily for hours. Sometimes days. Floodwaters can cause people to drown or buildings to crumble. The main health hazards during monsoon season are diseases like cholera, dengue, chikungunya, and malaria, as well as stomach and eye infections. While the torrential rains are similar to a hurricane, which can affect the islands in the Caribbean, a monsoon is not a single storm; it is a seasonal wind shift over the region. The shift can cause heavy rains in the summer months, but at other times it may cause a dry spell.

I am thankful that our taxi driver is so skilled and able to navigate the flooded streets. I notice today that many of the staff do not take home their laptops; they lock them in their desks, lockers or cupboards. I suppose it makes little sense to trot around with laptops if there is no Wi-Fi at home.

As part of Fun Week there is a gift exchange today. I feel ill-prepared as I didn't realise we were supposed to exchange gifts. The price range for the gift is K2,000. I have a Barbados flag pin that I can give to someone which easily costs more than K2,000. Khing Sa tells me that he wants to exchange with me. I hope he gets the pin, but this will only happen if I can manage to pull his name from the bag. I go with Adam to the supermarket to get his gift and some wrapping paper for our gifts. It is raining so I take my umbrella. On the way there he comments that he can't get over how beautiful my shoes are in comparison to the dirty surroundings. The streets are even dirtier once the rains have passed and all manner of debris lies on the sidewalks and the streets. He ends up settling on a pocket dictionary which has English and Burmese translations. It is exactly K2,000. I then explain to the lady in the store that we need wrapping paper and she takes me to it. Adam, whom I now refer to simply as "A", thinks they understand my accent better than his. We make our way back to the office and I wrap the gifts. I really hope Khing Sa gets his wish since he is such a sweetheart. Htun Htun and Than Tun are missing today because they are attending management training. I am so happy for them. Than Tun is a bright young fella and I am happy to see my senior lawyer Htun Htun progress. He is like my right hand and he is the gentlest man I have ever met. His wife is a lucky woman. Perhaps he will take me to meet her one day.

I see Badrick heading to the lunchroom and he comments that he can't believe it is after 12 p.m. already. Adam sees him too and takes this opportunity to tell me that he cannot understand Badrick's accent. I understand where Adam is coming from since I do not always understand it myself. The Jamaican accent is strong and there are usually subtitles when they speak on television as most people struggle to understand what they are saying. Badrick gives me a knock and says,

"Caribbean people". I am happy that he is happy I am here. It is lunch time and Elliot and Adam go out to get something to eat, but I am not in the mood to go with them. I want to be on my own today. I need some peace and quiet to be alone with my thoughts. I wait about 10 minutes and then I go to the Yangon Bakehouse.

I really like this little place. The items on the menu are really good, but what I also love about the Bakehouse is that it is a social enterprise that is dedicated to creating job opportunities for disadvantaged women. The restaurant and the catering business provide on-the-job training for the ladies as well as generate revenue to sustain the training programme. These disadvantaged women, made up of those from poor backgrounds with minimal education who lack stable incomes, are recruited by the bakehouse for a seven-month multiskilling training programme that provides culinary skills for employability. In addition, they get the opportunity to learn life skills related to healthcare and financial decision-making. When their training period is up, they are assisted in securing placement across cafés, restaurants and bakeries. I would eat here most days if I could, but it is always full. There is also the fact that because the offerings are good you will invariably run into someone from the office.

I manage to get a seat today and because of the close proximity of the seating — you basically share tables — I meet BB who is a World Bank consultant. When I first saw him, I thought he may have been a professor, but I suppose he could fit the NGO type as well. As we chat, I learn that he lives in Cambodia but is originally from Ohio in the US and his colleague who is with him is from Colombia but she lives in Luxembourg. They are working on a development project here in Yangon and of course had to come and support the Yangon Bakehouse. I tell him I am an attorney-at-law from Barbados and, when he asks, I explain how long it takes me to get from Barbados to Yangon. BB tells me he is interested in learning about the private sector and he gives me his email address, but I don't think that I will email him. I am too busy with my own work and have enough going on. I don't want to get roped into another project.

As I get setttled back in the office, Jane — who works in another department — tells Adam that she is going out and asks if he wants a burger. He says that he has already grabbed something with Elliot. She is always commenting on how skinny I am and saying I need to eat more, yet she does not offer to get me anything and I am sitting at the desk right across from Adam. I think you understand what I mean now when I said the expat women haven't warmed up to me. Perhaps she doesn't think I eat or that I have an eating disorder so I would be offended if she offers me a burger. Perhaps I am being overly sensitive. I am glad that I have already eaten.

As I am sitting at my desk working, out of the blue Ben, a former colleague, messages me. Ben is from Australia and was working with me in Barbados before he decided to take a year off from work to travel. Back then he had plans to rent a Mustang and drive cross-country in the US and do a tour of Asia. Before he left Barbados, he was encouraging me to sell my car and join him on his globe-trotting adventure. I was only a little tempted at the time. I was considering my career and my pockets and didn't feel that either could sustain any breaks.

I was just thinking of you the other day and wondering where you are. 1:50 PM

In Burma, you mean? 1:51 PM

Were you? ☺ I'm in Hanoi, Vietnam at the moment. 1:51 PM

No one calls it Burma anymore…it is Myanmar… Anton is here too. 1:53 PM

OK ok. Myanmar 1:53 PM

What do the locals call it? 1:54 PM

1:54 PM And Padhraic

I am teasing about the name. Call it what you want. The locals call it Myanmar. 1:54 PM

Yeh, I know Anton is there… tempted to drop in for a visit. 1:55 PM

I thought Padhraic was down in the Pacific somewhere. 1:55 PM

1:55 PM Yes, come

I'm touring Vietnam…3 weeks down, one to go 1:55 PM

Padhraic is based in PNG, but he is here on secondment too 1:55 PM

Then probably head to Thailand…Phuket and all the little islands 1:56 PM

I'd have to check on how easy it is to get a visa for Myanmar 1:56 PM

How long you there for? 1:56 PM

You can easily get a visa for
Myanmar in Bangkok. 1:56 PM

1:56 PM Here for 3 months initially

But we will see how it goes.
You know how these
things go sometimes. 1:57 PM

Only an hour on a plane from
Yangon to Phuket...come visit.
1:57 PM

1:57 PM This is my second week in.

Ok...how is the place? 1:57 PM

Why is so much going on there?
1:58 PM

1:58 PM I got my visa in KL

1:58 PM A project

Ok 1:59 PM

Are you enjoying the change of
scenery? 1:59 PM

1:59 PM Absolutely

1:59 PM Enjoying it

Nice 2:00 PM

Good to hear 2:00 PM

I was set to try and
move there 2:00 PM

There are two guys who are
from New Zealand but lived in
Melbourne here
2:00 PM

Bloody Kiwis! 2:00 PM

Keep them away from
the sheep 2:01 PM

They could probably find something for you to do here...lots of activity

2:01 PM

2:01 PM Talk to Anton

Haven't spoken to him in a while 2:01 PM

So who told you I was here? Lol
2:02 PM

Mary 2:02 PM

2:02 PM Oh ok

I still keep in touch with her and Rodney 2:02 PM

2:03 PM Cool

2:03 PM Well stay in touch

2:03 PM Going into a meeting now

They don't speak a lot of English
2:04 PM

Lol 2:04 PM

Good luck! 2:04 PM

But we have a translator who sits with legal
2:04 PM

I'm guessing you don't speak a lot of "Myanmarese" 2:04 PM

He learnt his English from the movies. American movies
2:04 PM

Lol 2:05 PM

2:05 PM Of course not

Does he have an American accent? 2:05 PM

No, slightly British .... he is great.... especially when he breaks.... 2:06 PM

2:06 PM Out in his own language

2:06 PM Later...

Lol 2:06 PM

Take care 2:07 PM

Say hi to Anton. Chat later 2:07 PM

2:07 PM Ok

I immediately go over to where Anton sits to tell him that Ben said hello. He says if he knew Ben may be coming he would have extended his time here. I am thinking Anton is leaving at the end of June so there is still time. When I get back to my desk, an email pops up inviting me to Anton's "Leaving Myanmar" dinner tonight. It is only now that our conversation about him extending his time makes sense.

At the office gift exchange I get a *Tom and Jerry* rice lunchbox. Adam gets a crab clock and is happy with it, considering he gave a dictionary. The girl who got my pin is wearing it on her sweater. Khing Sa gets a pink bra. I am thinking I should exchange with Khing Sa, but I do not think this is permitted. He may not like a yellow *Tom and Jerry* lunchbox. Khing Sa is not pleased with his pink bra and throws it on a vacant desk. The others are laughing. It sounds like Win Tin is telling him in Burmese to put on the bra tomorrow and wear it to work. I am dying with laughter. It is funny making up what I think they are saying.

ONYX

Friday, June 13, 2014

Last night was Anton's going away dinner at Onyx Restaurant. To get to the restaurant, we took a twenty-minute taxi ride from the office. The taxi driver dropped us off in a narrow alley and we walked through a muddy track to the restaurant. I silently cursed myself for not wearing rubber boots while I tried to walk gingerly on tiptoe so as not to get the mud on my shoes.

Onyx is a little hole-in-the-wall place which specialises in steak at dirt-cheap prices — a steak cost less than K15,000 or US$15. I had read some reviews about Onyx which were mixed and ranged from glowing to outright poor, but I was pleasantly surprised when I got to the place and found that it was not packed but at a comfortable capacity for the waiters to be attentive. From a cursory sweep of the room I noticed that the customers were made up of mostly expats with one or two Asians in business suits. They were probably Chinese or Japanese since there wasn't a longyi in sight except for those worn by the waiters. The place was lively, yet it had a cosy, intimate, unpretentious feel with low lighting. The mismatched furniture and slightly dirty tablecloths on a few of the tables in its old colonial building gave it a rustic feel. There were about seven of us in total and the waiter dragged two tables together so we could all sit together. I sat next to Anton. The menus were in plastic folders which were slightly greasy to touch. I took a deep breath, tried to put my germaphobia and cautious reactions related to the food in Yangon out of my mind and tried to enjoy myself. We talked and laughed while I drank red wine and ate pepper steak, well done (still not adventurous enough to have it any other way), vegetables and potato wedges. I was in good spirits. After dinner we went to Mojo for another round of drinks. By the time Adam and I made it back to the hotel around 11 p.m. I was very tired. The alarm went off at 5:30 a.m. as usual and I did not want to get up. I had started sleeping through the monk's drumming. I turned it off and continued to lie down until 7 a.m.

I learn this morning that some of our sites in Nay Pyi Taw are being vandalised. Whoever did it knew what they were doing, so it is not really vandalism; it is really sabotage. The police report is being translated into English by Than Tun, our official translator. This is just a regular day at the office. Vlado, who works as a systems architect in the Technical Department and who is from Serbia, invites Adam and me out tonight to a karaoke bar, I think. He says a group of them, locals included, is going. Apparently, the locals love karaoke. It feels like we are always going out. I didn't go out this much in my home country. I suppose it is only if you are anti-social that you will find yourself alone with nothing to do. What else am I going to do? Go back to my hotel room?

Ba Maw, who I think works in site acquisition, gives me two candy coins. He is the cutest. He is always saying hello and making sure I get things to eat. He reminds me of my little brother. The karaoke bar plans get cancelled because Su, who was going to come with us, has to go out to a site. I am thankful because I am very tired and just want a quiet evening in. I finally get back to the hotel and I order a bottle of wine and the chicken curry.

DALA TOWNSHIP AND
THE RICKSHAW DRIVER

Saturday, June 14, 2014

I see an email from Auntie Ann when I wake up. It is the first email that I have gotten from her since I have been here. She asks how I am doing but mostly she is reminding me that my mother's birthday is on Sunday. I didn't forget, but I don't know how I will call her since international calls don't work properly here and are hugely expensive. I feel like I constantly have to explain that to people.

I wish my mother would get WhatsApp or Blackberry messenger instead of relying on international calls for us to stay connected. We could even use Skype. Even though the Wi-Fi can be a bit sketchy it is still way better than landline international calls.

I am happy to hear from my aunt but also a bit annoyed. Based on the email from her, my family back home seems to think I should make a greater effort to maintain contact with them. However, I don't think they understand that Myanmar has only recently begun to open up to the world and, besides over the internet, it isn't as simple as picking up the phone and calling. When I woke up, I was not in the frame of mind to go into the office and this email does not make it any better. However, I drag myself up and begin the process of preparing for work, even though it is Saturday. I am going in today largely because Htun Htun, my right hand, is coming in. Htun Htun has two girls ages ten and two years old. If he has to make the effort to come, surely I can get up off my ass, eat my breakfast and make my way to the office as well. When I get there, I realise that the construction team is drilling. Oh great! I wonder if the air conditioner is working today because it seemed to not be working last Saturday when I was in. Maybe it is a Saturday thing. Now this will be productive, I think to myself.

Later in the day, I have a chat with the CEO who is also in today and he asks that I accompany him to a meeting with a potential new customer on Monday. I have some documents about the potential customer to read in preparation, of course, but I will do that tomorrow because Adam and I are going to the Dala Township after work this afternoon. I take a break from the work on my desk to look it up on Google. The extract doesn't say much: "Dala Township is located on the southern bank of the Yangon River across from downtown Yangon, Myanmar. The township, consisted of 23 wards, is bound by the Yangon River in the north and east, the Twante Canal in the west and Twante Township in the south. Despite its strategic location across downtown Yangon, the township is still largely rural and underdeveloped mainly because it still lacks a bridge across the Yangon River to downtown. Dala has 16 primary schools and one high school."

Yeah! I am usually game for an adventure. I am excited. But how will I finish all that I need to finish before then? I tell Htun Htun that I am going to Dala and he asks why I would want to go there. He says there is no running water over there and the only way to get there is by ferry. I am happy that I spoke to Htun Htun about the township because I am even more curious to see it now and I am still excited about experiencing all the adventure has to offer. After all, I am only in Myanmar for three months with no way of knowing if I would ever be back. I want to make the most of it and that included visiting the Dala Township this afternoon. However, when I get back to the hotel, I pack bottled water and all kinds of things in my bag, even Band-Aids, in case something happens and we cannot get back for the night. Adam and I have a taxi summoned for us and the taxi takes us to Pansodan Ferry Terminal in downtown Yangon. It is a twenty-minute ride from our hotel. When the taxi deposits us on the sidewalk, we head inside the ferry terminal and are ushered to the ticket desk for foreigners. The fee for the ferry is K2,000 to go and K3,000 to return and the ferry runs every ten minutes, so we don't have to wait too long for its arrival. Adam and I join the hundreds of people waiting to board the ferry. The crowd is made up of vendors with baskets and trays, monks with shaved heads and maroon-coloured robes, students, a few nuns in pink robes and people who I assume live in Dala. There are very few westerners like us waiting to board the ferry. When I ask Adam why there aren't more westerners like us, he explains that they take a tourist boat. I am happy we are taking the ferry to get an authentic experience. When the ferry arrives, there is no pushing and shoving and boarding is surprisingly done in an orderly fashion. Perhaps it is the years of military rule which makes boarding so orderly, I think to myself. We walk through a small turnstile and the ticket collector takes our ticket and gives us back our return ticket which we are careful to put away safely, lest the ticket office on the other side is closed and we are unable to make it back. The crossing is short and the river is calm enough to not make me want to throw up and lasts roughly ten minutes.

We arrive in Dala around 3:30 p.m. As we disembark the ferry, a sea of male and female fruit and fish vendors wearing bamboo hats greets us. Some of them have a few teeth missing and are squatting, while others, with faces wrinkled by the sun, sit on stools on the jetty selling their goods. Rows of small, wooden, brightly-coloured fishing boats are docked nearby on the river banks. As we leave the jetty, a minibus terminal and rows of taxis and rickshaw drivers are to our right. We had decided to just walk so we could take it all in, but a rickshaw driver convinces us to hire him. He tells us that he is from Dala and can show us all the best spots.

Dala is surreal. The houses are straw and bamboo huts and are built on stilts for when the flood waters come. Barely clothed children and a few naked ones are running around outside their homes and bathing in the river. The first stop is a monastery. As we make our way to the monastery, the rickshaw driver shows us a pile of sticks and tells us this was one of the sites of the 2008 cyclone where the death toll was over 4,000. I am wearing shorts, so I have to put on my longyi which I packed in my bag. Inside, we see the monks in their maroon-coloured robes walking in single file while clutching silver and enamel bowls in their hands. The rickshaw driver tells us that they are probably going to eat supper and are not likely to eat again until morning time. I am amazed by the scenes of Dala: children running in the mud chasing chickens and only stopping briefly to wave at us, cows roaming the muddy footpaths freely, ladies in their doorways weaving baskets or preparing a meal for their families, men and women side by side in longyis and bamboo hats in the paddy fields tending to the country's most important crop. As I gaze over at the men and women, the rickshaw driver tells us that is monsoon rice. It is sown in mid-June and transplanted in mid-July to be harvested in October. When they said it was rural, they were not kidding. Yangon is by no means a wealthy city, but the poverty in Dala is very noticeable. There are some serious National Geographic scenes. We see a water pump for the village that was funded by the European Union. I am curious and ask our driver what his life is like in Dala. He is the oldest in his family at twenty-one years old and he is already married. I see a girl who could be no more than 15 and she is carrying a baby. The people seem happy despite their circumstances. The rickshaw driver asks me if I am okay because outside is hot and I start fanning myself with my hands. I tell him I am fine. I was happy just getting to experience this place.

We finish our ride in about 2½ hours, after having to stop briefly and seek shelter in a tea shop because the rains came pouring down and the rickshaw driver, who, up to that point, I had thought was so nice, tries to extort US$25 each from us. We give him US$25 for the two of us, even though we had agreed to US$21 for both of us and he does not want to accept the money. He says we can keep it. I hold the money in my hand as we walk to wait for our ferry. He and a group of other Burmese men follow us to the jetty as a ferry is just pulling away. One says we are being unfair. I am getting upset now. I tell him this is all the money we have so he can take it or leave it since US$25 each is not what we had agreed. I remind him that we are going to walk, and he finally concedes, takes the money and leaves us alone. We continue to wait on the jetty for the next ferry which doesn't take long to arrive. Perhaps I had idealised the place and the people, but my grandmother always used to say, "You shouldn't let one bad eddo spoil the bunch."

MUM'S BIRTHDAY

Sunday, June 15, 2014

Today is my mother's birthday, but I could not call her. As I mentioned before, international calls are hugely expensive and they don't work properly in any event. My little brother, who is 15 years younger than I am, has not downloaded Skype on the computer yet. I probably should have done it before I left. I have asked Uncle Michael and Keisha to call her for me.

I sleep in late and make plans to do nothing today. I eventually go down to breakfast and, when I enter the dining area, I am mildly concerned that I have not seen my waiter Khing for several days now. As I eat, I casually scan the wait staff to see if he is among those on duty this morning, but I do not see him. I know he could not be off duty for several days in a row and I hope that nothing serious has happened to him. After breakfast I decide to visit the front desk to ask about Khing and one of the girls is able to explain to me in her limited English that Khing got a new job closer to home and has resigned. I am sad that he left without saying goodbye, but at the same time I am happy for him that he has secured better employment that would allow him to be closer to his family.

I go up to resume my sleeping and I remember Carlton's story about how he slept the entire weekend when he was at university. However, his sleeping away the entire weekend was for a different reason. He told me that when you sleep, you don't have to eat and while he was in university in Canada it was very hard on his family and he didn't have lots of money so he slept the entire weekend so he wouldn't have to eat. He later became a wealthy man and was able to retire in his 30s. My sleeping, though, is because I am genuinely tired. It is a lazy day and I am absolutely grateful.

Around 11 a.m., just after I woke up from my second nap for the day, I hear a knock on my door. It is housekeeping ready to service my room so I make my way to the hotel's lobby where I see Evan on his way to the restaurant. He spots me and comes over to where I am sitting and asks me if I will have a drink, but I decline. It is too early for a drink. Nevertheless, he sits with me for a bit and we have a chat. He tells me he has been to the office, despite it being Sunday and Father's Day, and not too many people are around. He talks about his children. He has a 20-year-old daughter in the UK who has just made him a grandfather, two kids in Kenya, one in Uganda and one in Thailand. He is an international dad. He asks if I miss my family and I tell him that I do, but not too much. I miss them mostly on Sundays as that is when I would drive over to my Auntie Ann's so we could have lunch together, but I have only been here two weeks so I will give it time. I tell him it is too busy during the week to miss them. We chat a bit more and then I tell him I will see him later in the evening. Back in my room, I order room service for lunch, read and take a nap.

I contemplate ordering room service again for dinner when I wake up, but I decide that I should go down and see people. I take the stairs so I can scope out who is sitting outside. I see the South African on the small dining terrace outside near the front of the hotel so I make a beeline for the dining room. I am not going to sit outside once the South African is there. I eat dinner alone, but it doesn't bother me in the least; I eat dinner alone at home most nights in Barbados. The difference here is I don't have to put it in the microwave; the chef at the hotel prepares it for me.

3 WEEKS IN

Monday, June 16, 2014

This is now the start of my third week. I took the taxi by myself this morning. This is the first morning I have not had the guys with me. As I get more accustomed to life in Yangon it is nice to make some moves on my own. Noah is still in Bangkok doing his visa run, having left last week, and Adam is crashing at Elliot's apartment since he and his wife Bea are in Scotland. I still haven't met Bea since she was in Thailand for a period engaged in training for teaching English as a foreign language, but I am sure I will meet her at some point. The solitude is good. I arrive at the same time as Ava and we exchange pleasantries.

"Wake Me Up" by Avicii is playing on the radio as I enter the lobby. I am not speaking too much this morning as I am not in the mood to chit chat. Whether it is in Myanmar or Barbados or St. Lucia, Monday morning blues are still very real. Is it lunch time yet? Breakfast has barely passed and I am already thinking about lunch. I think I will go to the French bakery today for lunch to get away. I know most of my colleagues skip the French bakery because of the walk and the price compared to other options around. I wish that they served soup at the French bakery. I am craving some warm soup as I think I may be coming down with something. My throat is sore and I feel very cold today. I really hope that how I am feeling today is just part of my Monday blues and not a sign of something more serious, especially as I have the meeting with the CEO at 1:30 p.m. Adam seems to think the meeting will largely be a commercial meeting. If that is the case, this should take me out of the office for a couple hours.

As I will be here for three months, I explore the idea of moving into an apartment and getting out of the hotel. I speak to Ava in HR. I have my doubts that I will find anywhere suitable as nice apartments that meet Western standards are scarce and very expensive here. I guess I will be staying at the hotel.

We are scheduled to leave the office for our meeting with the potential customer at 12:30 p.m. so that we will be on-time for a 1:30 p.m. start. When I glance at my watch, I realise that it is already 12:15 so it seems like I won't get to eat before the meeting. Instead of going to the bakery, I prepare myself for the meeting by visiting the washroom and gathering my handbag and notebook. Then I head down in the elevator. The CEO's driver meets us downstairs and we are off.

* * *

The meeting with the potential customer is positive. It lasts about an hour and a half and I have some actions that I jot down in my notebook for the team. By the time we make it back to our office it is about 4:30 p.m. I have a quick coffee and I send out the meeting notes and the actions to the team and, before I know it, it is already 6 p.m. As I reach the hotel, I notice that Noah and Evan are on the outside terrace having a sundowner. I stop and chat briefly with them primarily about Noah's visa run to Bangkok and then I make my way upstairs to my room. I just want to crash.

When I get to my room, I see a message from my stepmother. We have become close over the years after I spent several successive summer and winter holidays in the U.S. with them and they visited me on their trips to Barbados. She and my father are having a conniption because they have not seen any posts from me for a couple days. I explained that on Saturday I got back to the hotel late and the Wi-Fi has been even slower than usual. I reassure them I am fine and I didn't die in a far-off place.

Tuesday, June 17, 2014

When I reach the office, I see Adam who looks like something the cat dragged in. When I ask him what was wrong, he says he seems to have caught another stomach bug. He spent last night at Elliot's apartment but decided to return to the hotel. I give him some rehydration salts that I brought from Barbados (my doctor insisted I bring them) and hope he feels better. I am not sure what he ate, but he always goes experimenting. He and Than Tun went to a meeting yesterday and Than Tun thinks it may be because he had eaten late. I pray to God that I do not get sick here.

Mima, who is on holiday, texts me to remind me that she will be back to work on Thursday and that I am in her thoughts. She is such a sweet girl. The day just races by. I collect lunch from the Yangon Bakehouse and eat at my desk. I had hoped to go to the French bakery but didn't want to chance it in the rain. The French bakery is my little respite here in Yangon. I must remember to take a picture of it.

Evening finally comes and it is time to go home. I like that the taxi men outside the office know me now and they are ready to take me as soon as I emerge. When I exit the office building, I approach the group of taxi drivers positioned close to their lined-up vehicles chatting and

I tell them the name of my hotel and they say, "Yes, yes I know." I don't know what discussions they have among themselves. I get "home", shower and order room service. The TV feed is not too great, but I am able to get CNN and Al Jazeera. I suppose that is all I need. I check the list that Anton emailed to me on the top five things he liked about Yangon to see what my next adventure in Yangon should be. The five items on Anton's list are: Shwedagon Pagoda, Kandawgyi Nature Park, Chinatown, Bogyoke Aung San Market and visit a tea shop. I should probably try and do something productive, but I just want to sleep.

LANGUAGE LESSON

Wednesday, June 18, 2014

I am not in such a good mood today. Adam is out again. Communication with the team is still a big issue and Than Tun and I have not started my language lessons yet, but we are supposed to start this evening. About 40% of the time, I do not understand what Htun Htun is telling me and his English is the best of the lawyers.

Htun Htun brings me his overtime sheet to sign. I am not even sure what he is claiming, but I sign it because I know I can't afford to upset him or lose him. I would be lost if I do. I had told him yesterday that he should sit where I am sitting when I am gone. I want him to be thinking about the next step and the next promotion. He is very good.

Jane stops by for a brief chat. She enquires about Adam and is generally pleasant. She says I look pretty today and I thank her. Nu Nu, one of the members on my team of lawyers, scans my passport for me. I am glad that she does, because I take this opportunity to send it to my aunt so that she has a scan of the entire thing in case anything happens to me while I am here. I should have done this several weeks ago when I first arrived, but it only crossed my mind recently.

My next move is also on my mind. I love the team, but I have to think about whether it makes sense for me professionally and financially to be here longer than the three-month period I signed up for. Plus, I miss the beach. For the first time since I have been here, I miss the beach. I took for granted our white-sand beaches and clear crystal waters in Barbados. It was a privilege many people don't get to enjoy and tourists have to pay good money for.

In the elevator as we were making our way to the office this morning, Noah told me that he has moved out of the hotel and has gone to Hotel Grand United Ahlone which is about 15 minutes away from my hotel and 20 minutes from the office. He was having cabin fever at our current hotel and wanted a change of scenery. I wonder if it is nice. The staff at the hotel is familiar with me and is very helpful. I don't know that I want to have to go and get accustomed to another bed, another set of staff and a different commute.

The office is noisy today. The jackhammer is going and U Nu is very loud on the phone, but he normally is regardless of if the jackhammer is going or not.

* * *

I just had my favourite part of the day. It was nice outside, so I took a walk to the French bakery. It is hard to believe that a place like this exists in Yangon. It is so clean, they make the best salads that I have ever had and the staff members are lovely. My respite. The US$3-a-day lunch that I was told about when I was first preparing to come to Yangon is a myth. Well, not exactly. You can get a meal for US$3 a day or less, but this is at local places and you do so at your own risk. The salad costs K5,000 and the cappuccino costs K3,000 which amounts to a total of US$8. I know that I will be starving again by 4 p.m., but I like the place. Plus, I can't have soup and salad or soup and a half wrap three days in a row from Yangon Bakehouse. I have to pace myself or I will become tired of the food. I convince myself that by having the salad I am eating healthy.

Around 3 p.m. we are all called into the boardroom to congratulate a co-worker whom I don't know on being the Star of the Month. Good for him. As I sit back down at my desk, I see an email asking me to formulate a legal position on a matter we received from the Kayin and Mon states. I work on this until it is time for me to have my language lesson.

At 6:30 p.m. I have my first language lesson with Than Tun and he starts by explaining that the Burmese or Myanmar script was developed from the Mon script, which was adapted from a southern Indian script during the 8th century. The earliest known inscriptions in the Burmese script date from the 11th century. The rounded appearance of the letters is a result of the use of palm leaves as the traditional writing material. Straight lines would have torn the leaves. The Burmese name for script is "ca-lonh", meaning "round script". Burmese is a tonal language with three main tones (high, low and creaky) and two other tones (stopped and reduced). We start with the numbers as the alphabet may be too difficult at this stage. Adam is still in the office after we finish our first class and he thinks that the entire lesson sounded hilarious.

"NGA BAR LOTE YA MA LELL?" — WHAT AM I TO DO?

Thursday, June 19, 2014

I go down for breakfast a bit late. When I woke at 3 a.m. to go the bathroom, I realised my running partner in Barbados had messaged me to ask how it was going and I ended up chatting with him via WhatsApp for a bit. I haven't been running at all in Yangon. I am too afraid to get lost, bitten by a dog or run over by a car.

At breakfast, a Nigerian lady asks if she can join me. I suppose she is surprised to see another black person. She tells me her name is Mimi. Her skin is darker than mine and she is wearing braids. She is absolutely beautiful. I suppose she must get many stares here. I welcome her to my table. She tells me she lives in Bangkok, but she is in Yangon for training at the hotel and is leaving tomorrow. She works for Oxfam, which is a global organisation dedicated to ending poverty. I am pleased to meet another woman who is doing something meaningful with her life. She says this must be very different to what I am used to and I agree. It is a shame that we do not have more time to chat as I have to rush off to work and her training finishes tomorrow. I would have been very interested in hearing her story. Perhaps I will see her this evening, but I have serious doubts. Yangon is like that. Everyone is passing through.

In the taxi on my way to work, I look back at the words Than Tun has taught me. As the taxi drops me off, Badrick, the Jamaican, is arriving at the same time and he winds down his window and greets me with, "Morning, beautiful" and waits for me as my taxi has dropped me off a short distance from the door. He enquires about my well-being and what I do in the evenings. I tell him that I go out sometimes and sometimes I stay at the hotel. He says that I must invite him out one of these evenings and asks for my number. I do not know my number by heart and I have no plans of learning it. I tell him I will email it to him once I get to my desk, but I know that I will not because I don't feel like being pestered and I have a feeling he will pester me since he is always trying to "chat me up". We arrive at our office floor and part ways.

I am having a pretty good morning. I am practicing the words that Than Tun has taught me from my class yesterday and every time I say them the team erupts with laughter. I am not sure if they are laughing at me or laughing with me, but I am encouraged by the fact that I am able to make them laugh. One of the tasks for the day is an addendum to a lease. I could probably do it in five minutes, but I ask Htun Htun to get one of the junior lawyers to do it. He could probably do it as well, but I want the junior lawyers to develop. I have my three months here cut out for me.

Adam had to go to a meeting in Nay Pyi Taw with Su since Elliot is away. Poor Adam. Su was to pick him up from the hotel at 5:30 a.m. and the drive takes about 5 hours. I have had to wake up early plenty times to travel in the Caribbean and I am happy to have a break from that. It is not so much the travel as it is the early check-in followed by the waiting and delayed flights. As I sit at my desk, I remember a conversation I had with a colleague from the Caribbean office last year when he said he had no desire to go to Myanmar. Yes, the traffic is bad, the place is dirty and you have to be careful not to step in betel nut spit, but, those minor inconveniences aside, I do not clearly understand the reluctance to be here. The place is growing on me.

Htun Htun and Than Tun are going on training this morning at 9. "Nga bar lote ya ma lell?" What am I to do? Mima has returned from her holiday and brings me some traditional food from Mandalay. I want the entire legal team to help me eat the food, but she says that she has brought them some as well and they will eat theirs at lunch time. The gesture is so sweet, but it is a lot and I am not sure how I will eat it all. I ask Noah to try some and he comes and helps me a bit. He sits with me for a while and tells me about his new hotel and that his birthday is tomorrow. Noah says there is construction going on next to his hotel, so I tell him that it is a toss-up between the construction and the monks drumming. We laugh. I think I am getting used to the monks. I suggest we all go out for his birthday as tomorrow is Friday night and we make plans for the gang to go to the Sule Shangri-La Hotel and Mojo.

There is a lovely, garlicky scent coming from the lunchroom. The local staff are having their lunch. I pop in to get some water and I see a spread which includes an array of Asian food and they are all sharing with each other. Of course, there is rice. I go out to get my lunch from the Yangon Bakehouse with Noah. We chat about his plans to possibly work in the UK once he has finished his stint here in Yangon. I bring my lunch back to my desk and just as I am about to dive into my Greek salad Evan comes to my desk asking if I knew where Adam was. I tell him that Adam has gone to Nay Pyi Taw and ask if I can help. He explains that he fired a sub-contractor last night and the site manager called to tell him he shouldn't go to the site because the man he fired says he is going to kill him. Evan, who is quite macho, thinks he is bigger than the guy and can fight him. I ask him if it is absolutely necessary for him to go on the site and advise him that the site manager could be exaggerating but not to go to the site in any event. He is no use to us dead. My experience as legal and regulatory manager in Yangon is truly a unique one and I am grateful for it.

Ben messages me and reminds me that it is his 40th birthday today. He is in Phuket, Thailand at the moment. We joke that he has finally gotten around to taking his gap year. He says that his hotel is horrible and he is looking for a new one. He just finished touring Vietnam and he plans to spend a month in Thailand. He says I must go to Halong Bay and Sapa, both reachable from Hanoi, if I get a chance to visit Vietnam. But I tell him it is too early in my stint to take time off.

It is fun chatting with Ben, but eventually I wish him a happy birthday one last time and try to refocus on my task. However, I am struggling to do so. Neither Than Tun, Htun Htun nor Adam is here to keep my company and I find my attention waning. Noah sees me yawning so he suggests that we go for coffee. I jump at the offer and suggest we go to the French bakery. When we get there, there is only one vacant table left and we end up being seated next to a gentleman wearing a khaki shirt and pants and looking as though he just stepped out of an Indiana Jones movie. Because of the close proximity of the seating, he looks over and introduces himself. He tells us his name is Dave and that he works as an independent journalist for a TV news station. He is from New York and is here to train Burmese journalists. He had been here for five months before taking up this stint. He seems a little eccentric by his dress. While we sip our coffee, he chats about an interview he got with the Prime Minister of Bangladesh and about a protest that was staged in front of the Bangladesh Embassy. He asks us whether there will be a protest in front of the office of a Muslim-owned company and whether we think it would be peaceful. In Myanmar, because the country is largely Buddhist, there is an anti-Muslim sentiment among some members of the country which has led to protest action and is the basis for Dave's questions. Noah says there was a press release in the newspaper about that company's launch and we say that we don't think there will be a protest. Dave is a journalist, after all, and we do not want to have that type of political discussion with him in a country where we are merely guests. I can tell Dave is very passionate about what he does, but he seems to only be interested in protests. I tell him to visit Dala instead and report on the place so the people who live there can get a bridge. I suppose everyone has their own agenda here. He comments that this is the last time we will get to see an opening up such as this and says, quite sardonically, that the next one will be when they decide to open North Korea.

Just as we are about to leave, I realise there is some type of photoshoot taking place outside the French bakery. There is a small crew with tripods and other photography equipment standing outside and what seems to be a makeup artist fussing over a female model.

We head back to the office. I am awake now and I settle down to read some more about Burmese land law. Ba Maw comes back from the registration office, where he was registering some of our leases and brings me a key ring and an apple. He is just the cutest. I must be sure to take a picture of him before I leave.

Auntie Ann has now started sending me an email every day so that I can respond to it so she can be sure I am okay. I don't know if this is the best way for her to check on me as the Wi-Fi is really unreliable, but I will indulge her nevertheless. It is good that she wants to check on me. I can't see her visiting me here in Yangon, though, since she doesn't like long flights.

NOAH'S BIRTHDAY

Friday, June 20, 2014

Noah greets me as I alight from the taxi just in front of our office building. He seems to be in a particularly jubilant mood this morning and I am soon to be reminded of why – today is his birthday. I wish him a happy birthday and as we walk to the elevator Noah marvels at how much life has changed for him in the past year. He tells me that he was in New York this time last year. I smile and nod my understanding. Yangon is a far cry from New York. They are like chalk and cheese.

When I get to my desk, U Nu tells me that Ne Win is not well and he had to take a day's leave. I ask if it is the flu or a tummy ache. He explains that he is sick from sitting by the air conditioning. I don't know what to say. I was actually thinking how nice the temperature in the office was yesterday. It was not as cold as it usually is and I didn't need my sweater. I look around to see where I can ask Ne Win to sit when he returns to avoid a repeat of this. I can't have him being sick from the air conditioning. He is an important member of the team. Everyone wants to know when Adam is coming back from Nay Pyi Taw, but all I know is that he will be back sometime today since they couldn't drive last night. The roads are dangerous, especially in the rainy season, and there are lots of accidents.

I get a WhatsApp message from Auntie Ann's mobile number. It simply says, "Hi, this is Auntie Ann." When I reply I learn that it is really Uncle Michael setting up the WhatsApp for her. I am delighted that she will have WhatsApp soon since it means she can stop emailing. She isn't really into technology, but at least I will have another means to communicate with her. She is, after all, handling all of my affairs while I am here.

Padhraic comes and chats with me. He is excited about going back to Papua New Guinea (PNG). What was supposed to be six weeks for him here turned out to be close to six months. I know the same could happen to me — three months could turn into three years or more. He says that he thought about doing law and he enjoyed reading contracts as a component of his marketing degree, but his English writing is poor. It is always funny to me when I hear people express an interest in doing law when, sometimes, I think that I don't want to do law anymore. To those not in the legal profession, it is generally considered a well-respected career that will make you decent money and I am grateful to have found myself on the legal team of a good company; however, no one likes lawyers, especially the business units that you are there to help. Sometimes you ask yourself if it is really worth it. Sometimes it is only when the shit hits the fan that people start copying in the Legal Department on emails. I have to cut our chat short as I have to send an urgent email.

Su, Htet Htet who works in Noah's department, Adam, Elliot and I have lunch at a place called The Golden Duck. I figured it was an Asian restaurant by the name, but as it is Noah's birthday I don't want to insist on the French bakery. We have to sit upstairs because the place is packed. It looks like a typical Chinese restaurant with the round tables and lazy Susans in the middle. Noah says he loves the spareribs at The Golden Duck, and since I am feeling adventurous, I order some too. It is my first pork dish in Yangon. I have been avoiding the spareribs, sweet and sour pork, pork fried rice and pretty much any other pork dish so far. As I observe our waiter taking the orders at our table, I realise that he, Su and Htet Htet sound as though they are pronouncing it "pok", without the "r". I feel like every time I order in Asian restaurants here I am taking a risk — you are never sure what you will get, but you have to eat. Adam accidentally ordered snake head a few nights ago at another restaurant. When you order, you say a little prayer, hope that the food does not make you sick and you dig in.

Despite my usual apprehension about ordering meats from Asian menus, the spareribs are delicious. We spend a very pleasant hour of lunch and then head back to the office. I am typing at my desk when Badrick comes over to explain a legal problem he is having. During an excavation a neighbour's house was damaged and the contractor told him it will cost 3 lakhs to fix. We offer to repair the damage; however, the owner of the house does not want us to fix it and is demanding 50 lakhs, that is US$5,000. The village chief — it seems like nothing happens in any village in Yangon without the village chief getting involved — says he will get them to agree to accept US$3,000. However, I tell Badrick that we can't pay that kind of money and we begin to discuss the possibilities, but I can tell that Badrick's primary reason for visiting my desk may not have been related to the issue of the damaged house. He keeps prodding me to go out with him later for a drink. I am annoyed by Badrick's continuous attempts to make passes at me, especially now when there is an important matter to be dealt with. I am ready to buss out in my best Jamaican accent: *Rass claat... stop try fi put argument to me, man.... You can't 'andle me. You nah know who you a deal wid. Me nah easy.* But I refrain and instead I tell him to send me the details of the legal problem and he is promptly dismissed as I resume typing.

As I am heading back to the hotel in a taxi, I check my messages and realise that Sean, a colleague who worked with me in the Barbados office and who is now based in Ireland, sent me a WhatsApp message to see how I am doing. He asks if I am behaving and I reply with "Of course not". I tell him about Noah's birthday and the plans for later this evening. By the time the taxi driver drops me off, Keisha has also messaged me and I chat with her a bit. She is waiting to take a flight to go to see her mother and sister in Antigua. Keisha's mom is Antiguan and her sister, who lives in Canada, is also flying to Antigua so the three can spend some time together. The timing is perfect as it was a free ticket and she wanted a break from work.

* * *

I get to the bar at Shangri-La close to 8 p.m., a far cry from the 6:30 p.m. time on Noah's birthday invite. After work I went back to the hotel to shower and rest for a bit. Plus, I couldn't decide if I really wanted to go. When I arrive at the bar, I immediately spot the group and walk over to join them. I am sandwiched between Ava and Noah who claims they got there hours ago. Another South African who has been in Yangon for about a week is also at our table, along with Padhraic and Ava's friend Liam who is here on holiday. About ten minutes later Adam joins us and we place our orders for food together since it seems like everyone else has already eaten. It is a lively bunch and I am glad to be out. Soon after I get there, another friend of Ava's — Natasha who is from Poland — also joins us. She has very pale skin and is slim and petite with delicate features and blond hair. She explains that she in the field of hospitality and has been in Myanmar for a year. I wonder what area of hospitality she is in, but the bar is too loud for me to ask. They make room for her and both Noah and the new South African want to sit next to her. Badrick arrives and wishes Noah happy birthday and Jennifer joins us later. The guys don't make the same fuss over her as they did with Natasha. In contrast, Jennifer is Irish, tall and solidly built with a strong jawline and dark brown hair. I met Jennifer about a year ago at our office in Jamaica when she had only joined the company a few days. I remember that she had been sent to Yangon shortly after our meeting in Jamaica and I vaguely wondered why I hadn't seen her at the office yet. But I learn that she jumped ship early in her tenure and is now working for another company. We exchange pleasantries and I tell her how good it is to see her again.

When we get tired of Shangri-La, we decide to head over to Union Bar which is approximately a ten-minute drive away. Upon exiting Shangri-La, we realise that Jennifer's driver has been waiting for her, so five of us ride with Jennifer and the rest take a taxi behind us. I think the group may have grown to about ten or eleven persons by now. When we reach Union, I realise that we lost Badrick at some point along the way. I suppose he didn't wish to join us at Union. One of Natasha's friends also joins us, but I do not get her name.

This is my first time to Union Bar and Grill. The place is nicely lit and is bright despite the dark wood. A few TV screens are showing various sports even though it is not your typical sports bar. The décor is a mix of modern and colonial and the tables are surrounded by cane-backed chairs that are normally found in old plantation houses. There are high cane-backed chairs lining the bar area. The actual bar area is smack dab in the middle of the room and serves as a type of divider, separating the diners on the right and front from the mostly drinkers on the left and at the back. At the back there is a raised platform with tables of drinkers and smokers as smoking is permitted inside Union Bar. The atmosphere is lively. The waiter ushers our group to the back of the bar to a raised platform area and joins two tables for us so we can all sit together.

As soon as we settle into our seats, Noah amps up his celebrations. He orders several drinks from the bar and sings and dances to the music being played by the DJ who is stationed at the far end of the raised platform. I sit next to Adam sipping my dirty martini and watching as Noah has the time of his life. At some points he stumbles and I think he might topple over, but then he masterfully steadies himself and keeps going. Nelly's song "Hot in Here" starts up and Noah is uncontrollable. He sits on Padhraic's lap and unbuttons his shirt. Padhraic does not look particularly disturbed. In fact, he encourages him by adding his own dance moves to the mix. It is hilarious. Noah is definitely the life of the party.

Every so often Adam gives me a knowing look. I can tell that he has had enough and is soon ready to leave which suits me fine as I can only seem to take everyone in small doses. Only last weekend on the way to Dala Township we had a conversation about being too old for hangovers. Apart from the headaches and generally feeling like shit, the problem with hangovers is that you are not productive the next day and the entire day usually goes to waste. We take some pictures and I can tell Noah is getting drunk. Since the others are up dancing, I move to sit next to Adam.

Adam has been out of office a couple days this week so we haven't had time to catch up. He tells me he has to go get a check-up in Bangkok. He has very light skin and has developed some growths that he must attend to as they have the possibility of developing into skin cancer. I can tell that he is worried but trying to play it cool. I hope it is not too serious and I am also hoping that he does not jump ship. I tell him that I am ready to leave as soon as he is. He nods and explains to me that he has to make a stop at Elliot's apartment to collect his things and then head back to the hotel. We take a taxi there.

Elliot's apartment is in the thick of things and in a rough part of the city. The area is dark. I am not sure if it is because its residents have already gone to bed or if there is just a lack of electricity in that area. Some local men are gambling downstairs by a shop and a few stray dogs digging through garbage bins. I haven't been to this part of the city before; there has been no reason for me to come here. We take the elevator to the 8th floor. The apartment reminds me of the apartments I see on TV in the dodgy parts of New York that have huge metal gates with the crisscross pattern. We have to unlock about three padlocks just to get in. Despite the location, Elliot's apartment is very spacious and well-appointed. There are balconies off the living room and the bedrooms. The views are nice from up there. The contrast of the hundreds of stars in the pitch-black sky stands out to me. It feels weird being in Elliot's apartment when he is not here and even weirder that I am here with Adam. I look around and I see a picture of Elliot and his wife. She is pretty with short black hair, warm brown eyes and an endearing smile. I hope we get on when she gets back from Scotland and we can finally meet. The apartment is nice, but I couldn't see myself living in this part of town. We grab Adam's things and leave. I am thankful that the taxi driver waited, but I remember he would have waited in any event because we had not yet paid him. He charges K3,000 from Union Bar to Elliot's place and another K3,000 from there to the hotel. As we ride up the elevator to our respective rooms, Adam asks if I will do any touristy stuff this weekend. I tell him probably on Sunday. I'd like to visit Junction Square as I haven't been there yet. I am able to hit my bed just after 12 a.m.

BUILDING RELATIONSHIPS
AND MAKING CONNECTIONS

Saturday, June 21, 2014

A text from Noah wakes me up. It is around 8 a.m. I am surprised that he is awake, considering that he was acting very drunk last night and I was sure he would have a serious hangover that would cause him to sleep in. I wonder what time they left the bar last night. The text reads:

> *Morning. Hope you're ok. Apologies if I was an ass last night. Going to 50th Street later to watch rugby if you want to join.*

I respond an hour later telling him no worries and that I had a great time. I agree to visit 50th Street after leaving the office.

I get to the office and Mima is already there. I am glad I did not blow off going in. She kept her word so it would have been terrible if I hadn't kept mine. The Burmese lawyers are fully pimped out on Saturdays and there are no longyis in sight. They look very "Westernised" in their baseball caps and shorts, a stark difference from what I see during the week. They look like regular young people, even though their lives are probably far from regular. It is just after 10 a.m. and it seems like they have ordered takeout from somewhere and are sharing among themselves. I cannot help but observe Than Tun and San San. As I watch them, San San allows Than Tun to sit and begin eating before she does the same. I met San San, who is an engineer for the company, during my first week here. San San is very beautiful; she is a light-skinned Burmese with skin like a porcelain doll as opposed to a brown-skinned Burmese. She has delicate features and long black hair. She and Than Tun have developed a very close friendship and the two of them, along with Htun Htun, share a taxi in the evenings. I remember there was one evening when Than Tun had to stay late to finish his translations and she was urging him to come along. She did not want to go without him. During our Fun Week, Than Tun loaned or gave her money to participate in our World Cup sweepstakes. I know that Than Tun is in office today for training, but I am not sure why San San is here. They are very protective of each other.

The CEO, who is headed to the lunchroom, stops in the Legal Department and asks me how long I am staying today. When I tell him probably until 2 p.m., he asks if I will take the day off tomorrow, which is Sunday. Of course I will. Things are very busy, but I think a break and self-care are important. At 2:30 p.m. I get back to the hotel and change my LK Bennet flats to my MK ones and swap my large MK bag for my smaller Longchamp one. I wanted to lie down for a bit but changed my mind as I felt I should get out and meet people. I decide to make good on my earlier promise to Noah to join him and some others at the 50th Street Bar. Outside my hotel I jump into a taxi, give the taxi driver my destination and relax a bit during the short ride.

50th Street Bar is hard to miss. It is located in a two-storey yellow and white building with large brown doors and looks slightly out of place among the more traditional buildings. As I enter, I notice it is styled as a modern and Western pub with a wood-panelled bar, wooden floors,

TVs and a big screen projector, and drinking memorabilia from other parts of South East Asia on its brick walls. There is a group of expats playing pool and two other expats playing a game of darts. On the ground floor are booths and tables and chairs are set out for dining. When I arrive, Ava and Jennifer and some friends are sitting on the first level in a booth near the stairs. I politely say hello and I think that Noah may be upstairs, but as I am about to ask Ava if she has seen him, he texts me to say he is five minutes away and he has been having a fun day at Junction Square. I nevertheless make my way to the second level where there are several couches and lounge chairs and a stage area for when the bar has live bands. Noah arrives panting just as the game is about to start. He plops himself down next to me on the couch and we watch as the All Blacks play England. The crowd is very anti-England except for one guy with black hair whom I am yet to meet.

I go to the bathroom and when I return, I see another addition to the group whom I haven't met. Noah introduces us. Her name is Katherine and she is from the UK. She works for the company as well, but she went to have an operation, had some complications and has been away from work. She explains that she is tired being cooped up inside, so she came out to see the rugby. The All Blacks win the game and soon after that we move over to Katherine's table where I meet Matt who is tall and handsome with dark hair and I am immediately interested in what he does for a living as he states that he works in private equity. I want to know about the types of clients he has, whether he has worked on any high-stakes ventures, what types of hours he works, that kind of thing. William, whom I dated for close to four years, is an investment banker and I found his stories interesting so I imagined Matt would have even more interesting stories. Matt is British, which explains why he was the only one cheering for England. (Coincidentally, William is also British.) He says he is pretty settled in Myanmar and he has been here for ten months and lives near Scott's Market (the old name for Bogyoke Aung San Market). Matt, who has been sitting next to me, gets up for a few moments to go to the bathroom and Noah takes the opportunity to plop his ass down next to me. I am bummed out. I was really enjoying Matt's presence beside me and I wanted to continue learning about him. When Matt returns Noah does not relinquish the seat next to me. I wait Noah out a bit, but when I realise that he has no intention of moving, I tell him I have to meet up with friends and I make my exit. I will have to figure out how I will get to see Matt again to hear the rest of his story. Maybe I can connect with him again via Katherine in some way. Katherine has a boyfriend here in Myanmar who is friends with Matt and may know Matt's deal. She seems more friendly than Ava. She smokes and curses and swears like a pirate, is very blunt and seems like a badass, but I like her already. She seems real and unpretentious.

I get back to the hotel and I see a message from Noah asking how I am doing. I tell him that I am fine and I made it back okay even though the roads are flooded. I had a great afternoon. It is the monsoon period, so the flooded roads are a common thing in Yangon. I am spent after an evening of writing and I just go to bed. I don't even bother to take off my clothes. I am sleeping before I know it.

Sunday, June 22, 2014

For some reason I kept waking up during the night last night and checking my Barbados phone. There is not a message from a single soul. No one cares about me, I think to myself. I had a restless night last night. I am thankful that I will at least get to sleep in. I am beginning to miss yoga, but I still haven't been able to find a class here in Yangon. When I finally get out of bed it is close to 9 a.m. I go down to have breakfast and return to bed. I decide to sleep a little longer due to the restless night.

It is my hair wash day and as soon as I get up from my late-morning nap, I get right to it. The trials of being a black woman in Yangon. If I had been back in Barbados I would have just rolled up into the hairdresser's chair and have her do this for me. When I finally sort my hair out it is close to midday and I promised myself that I would check out Junction Square, so I prepare for my little solo excursion.

Junction Square is a mall located at the intersection of two main roads. When I reach, I am in good spirits. I walk around and make a mental note in case I run out of anything, especially red lipstick. The mall has three levels. Jewellery shops, an electronics store, a money changer, toy shops and clothing shops selling kids' clothing, Western and Burmese clothes are on the first level. Some of the shop tenants have brought their goods outside in front of the shops to entice customers in. The mall is packed with people — Asians mostly, and a few Western tourists — and is quite noisy. The food court is on the second level and a cinema is on the third.

Junction Square sort of reminds me of Trincity Mall in Trinidad and Sheraton Mall in Barbados, but only in the sense that the location of the stores is done in a very haphazard manner. There are mostly local shops and I do not spot any international brands. This is Yangon — a hodgepodge — nothing in any particular order, not at all organised or properly laid out. I decide that I will leave the shopping to when I travel to Bangkok for my visa run.

When I get back to the hotel, I glance over and see Evan is outside the hotel on the small outdoor terrace drinking and smoking. He doesn't see me, so I slip into the hotel lobby. The song "Summer" by Calvin Harris is playing on the TV in the lobby.

I think to myself that it is summer and I still haven't met anyone. Honestly, I didn't come to Yangon with the intention of meeting anyone, but I am not opposed to meeting someone. If I were to meet someone, and depending on how it goes, that may influence my decision on whether or not to stay in Yangon. In my room, I log into Facebook and I have a Message from God which says:

*Today, Nadia, we believe God wants you to know
that...letting go makes you wealthier. Wealth is never
measured by what you have, but by what you can give
away. You are rich with money when you can afford to
donate. You are rich with love when you can give love
freely. You are rich with God when you can behold
your enemy with compassion.*

Perhaps I am here in Yangon to learn to let go and love freely. Since things with William turned out to be a disaster, I have been very guarded with my feelings and who I let into my life, not just romantically. When I accepted this assignment, I had become more of a work machine than a human being, and I had seen Yangon only as an opportunity to advance in my career. However, the kindness I have experienced from my team of Burmese lawyers and the connections I have made with my little gang of fellow expats have caused me to relax and open my heart to people and experiences again.

THIS IS NOT MY HOME

Monday, June 23, 2014

Noah is missing from the office today. The others think that he may have "Yangon belly". I was told that during the rainy season in Myanmar, as the environment becomes more hospitable to viruses, food hygiene and water quality become more prone to bacteria and parasites that Yangon belly is common.

People suddenly have abdominal pain, diarrhoea, fever and fatigue. It doesn't help that he and Adam also like to experiment with food. I remember one of the locals telling me to be careful. She explained that their (the locals') stomachs are used to the food and water but because my stomach isn't, I could die. Of course, I thought she was being a bit dramatic about dying, but I heeded her advice, nevertheless.

Khing Sa has spent half the day writing something on a white board. Once he is done, he steps back and admires his handiwork. Even though I have no idea what he has written I can tell that he is proud of himself. I honestly do not think that anyone reads that board. I haven't read it myself.

It is only today when Su brought me a printout of a site and I wanted to contact her to request access to a soft copy that I realised no landlines are on the desks. I am reluctant to even move from my seated position because I am not feeling well, but I need to go to the department that Su is in so I can request the electronic copy. Today is the first day I felt truly sick since I have been here. I threw up all of my lunch. It was a disaster. I hope that I am not getting "Yangon belly" as well.

I look at the calendar and see that today is the trial date for a matter I was dealing with in St. Lucia. I take little comfort in the fact that I would rather not have to deal with a trial but here I am having trials of a different kind. I am in great pain; my stomach feels as though it is going to drop out. After work, I go straight back to the hotel, crawl into my bed and curl up in a ball. The electricity keeps going out, but the generator picks up the slack during the brief outages. Even though the air conditioning is at a comfortable temperature I am cold. I am terrified by the possibility that I am getting sick so far away from home and I pray hard that this is not what is happening. For the first time since I have been here, I desperately want to go home. I think of all the stress it would be on my family if I were to die, forcing them to come and collect my body and fly it back to Barbados. I resolve that I will not die here. I will make it back home. When I wake up it is 10:30 p.m. so I have missed dinner, but I am not sure what state my stomach is in. I call downstairs to room service and ask them to bring me some toast and tonic water to settle my stomach. I eat the toast and feel only slightly better. I eat nothing else for the rest of the night as I do not want to upset my stomach further. I go back to bed. Perhaps I will feel better in the morning. As I lie in bed, I remember a conversation I had with Olga, a former colleague in Barbados. She took her young daughter on a trip abroad and her daughter said, "This is not my home. I want to go home with you and Daddy and Emily." I now have some understanding of how she must have felt.

The alarm goes off at the usual 5:30 a.m., but I do not move. I finally crawl out of bed at 7:00 a.m. and I do not rush to do anything; if I am late, so be it. I finally get down to breakfast around 7:30 a.m. and Adam is arriving at the same time so he sits with me. I dare not risk eating anything but two slices of dry toast, a thin pancake with no syrup and some Lipton tea. Let us see if that stays down. I had tried somewhere different for lunch yesterday, but I threw up all my lunch. It was as though the universe was saying, "Do you see what happens when you try somewhere different?" I will take it easy on my stomach today.

NO WORK E-MAILS

Tuesday, June 24, 2014

I am feeling significantly better today and I am grateful for that. However, I am faced with a problem of a different kind in the office - my email stopped working at 11:00 a.m. without warning. I am able to send emails but not receive. The guy in the IT Department who comes to investigate says the link from Myanmar to Singapore may be down which would prevent me from getting emails. This is a disaster and will put a dent in my productivity today.

Emails are not even coming through on my phone. I have to enlist Than Tun to help me send emails through his email address and then write at the bottom: *Sent on behalf of Nadia whose email is not working.* I leave the office around 6 p.m. and when I get back to the hotel all the emails come flooding in on my phone. I start to read some, but then put down the phone so that I can rest my eyes for a few minutes. When I wake up it is 9:15 p.m. so I decide to go down to dinner since I would have to wait until morning to eat anything if I skip it.

As I am sitting in the dining room for dinner, I cannot help but notice an Asian young woman who looks about twenty-five and a much older white gentleman of about eighty years old occupying the table just across from me. I am not sure if they are guests at the hotel or if they just came to have dinner. She is wearing white shorts, bright red heels and a kimono-styled top. They are enjoying each other's company. I overhear her asking him if he wants dessert and he declines, but she says that she will go and check them out. She sashays over to the glass case that houses the desserts located at the entrance to the dining room, makes her selection and the waiter takes it back to her table. As she sits, our eyes meet and she smiles. The older gentleman orders a coffee and a whiskey. When they are finished, he pays the bill, she takes his hand and they leave the dining room. He is very happy with his young chick.

Two of Logan's friends — Mark and Lucia — email me to say they are in Bangkok at the moment but they live in FMI City. FMI City, one of Yangon's gated communities, is a bit far out of the city — about an hour's drive if the traffic is reasonable but much longer if it isn't. It is close to the Pun Hlaing Golf Club. We make plans to meet up when they get back to Myanmar.

LOSE ONE, GAIN TWO

Wednesday, June 25, 2014

IT is finally able to help me. A new guy comes and explains that the problem is an IP address which keeps knocking off the fixed IP addresses or something like that. I thank him and embark on the task of labouring through the many emails which have accumulated while I've spent practically the entire morning getting IT to fix my computer.

I am in a less than pleasant mood. Noah understands and he comes with me to the French bakery. I smile when the young lady at the counter asks if I am having the same salad I always order. I have officially become a regular.

Back at the office, it is near 5 p.m. and I catch Than Tun mocking Ava's pronunciation of 'Myanmar' and I can't stop laughing. He is so cheeky. It is the most hilarious thing. Maybe he is not fond of her either.

Padhraic is finishing up his stint today and we are going to Cask 81 — a whiskey bar — after work. However, I am not sure what time I will finish today as I am still catching up on emails. I finish around 6:30 p.m. and my usual taxi driver is waiting for me. I have to tell him that I am just going across the street to Cask 81 and not to the hotel. He says okay but seems disappointed. The truth is, I would prefer to go to the hotel as I still am not feeling 100% and I am not sure what awaits me behind the doors of Cask 81, but I want to be present to celebrate with Padhraic and wish him all the best on the next leg of his journey. I go to the restaurant first and I am redirected by the hostess there as the bar is in a building behind the Japanese restaurant. When I enter, I am not sure that I am still in Yangon. Inside looks swanky and chic. The bar has an industrial style. It is spotlessly clean with floor to ceiling windows, exposed beams, grey walls, tan leather couches and a long wall full of whiskey bottles. I am directed by the waiter to where my party is seated. When I get there, most of the gang is already present, even Evan. I am surprised that he is out but then I shouldn't be since drinking is involved. I chat with Jennifer and Ava and the new guy, Finn, who is from Ireland like Jennifer, Jane, Ava and Murray. Since I don't drink whiskey, I order a dirty martini. Present at Cask 81 is another new hire, this time from the Dominican Republic, but I don't catch his name as there is lots of chatter and cross-talking among the group. This is truly a multinational environment.

One of the South Africans joins us and ends up sitting next to me. He is probably the most palatable of the South Africans. I am forced to chat with him since he is sitting right beside me. He was in Thailand before coming to Myanmar and he has a multiple entry visa so he won't have to make visa runs like the rest of us. Alejandro and Adam finally arrive. I catch Evan looking at me out of the corner of my eye. He looks bored, but he always seems bored with everything. I observe the new Irish guy, Finn. He is about 6 feet 2 inches tall with black hair and refined manners. Could he be a potential? I am not entirely sure. He seems a bit smarter than those in the bunch, but it could also be that his novelty hasn't worn off yet. He has been with the company a year and has been based in Singapore and Fiji. Time will tell on his suitability. When we have had enough of Cask 81, we decide to move the party to Union Bar. Alejandro pays the bill. I don't think that Evan will join us since he thinks Union is too posh.

Adam, Ava, Finn and I ride with Jennifer and her driver. The rest get a lift with Alejandro and his driver who will pass Union on his way back to his hotel. At Union we see someone called Farrell and some other people whom Padhraic knows. Padhraic introduces us and Farrell pauses from smoking his cigarette briefly to shake my hand. I had only seen Farrell's name in emails before so this is the first time I am meeting him in person. He is also Irish. Union is busy and it is only Wednesday night. The waiter sets up a table for us on the raised platform area and I order a tonic water and the chicken and mushroom pizza. I have had enough dirty martinis.

I chat with Jennifer on where I can get a manicure and pedicure and she tells me about the local girl she goes to who operates in the Asia Light building. She also mentions that Union is more lively tonight than it was on Saturday night when she was here. She said on Saturday night it was dead, notwithstanding there was a DJ. She is enjoying life at her new company. I can tell, since she gets a driver and a nice pad. Noah and Adam later join us on the raised platform just as my pizza arrives. I am starving, but I can't possibly eat it all, so they help me. We chat some more and I think Adam picks up my cue that I am ready to depart. I leave some money with Noah for the bill and make a swift exit. When we get outside, another expat is haggling with the taxi driver to take her downtown for K1,500. We decide to haggle too and get our taxi driver to take us back to the hotel for K3,500, down from K4,000. When we get back to the hotel, we spot Evan outside smoking and drinking. However, I have certainly had enough socialising for one night, so I wave to him and Adam wishes me a good night and goes over to join him while I head upstairs to my room.

RETIRE YOUNG AND GET DIPLOMATIC PASSPORTS

Thursday, June 26, 2014

I wake up and finish the running convo I have been having with Karina via WhatsApp. Karina, who worked in the Sales and Marketing Department in Barbados as a business analyst, messaged me just before I went to bed last night to ask how it was going. At some point I fell asleep in mid conversation. She tells me the office there is the same. The former CEO who had moved to Jamaica is in Barbados for a workshop and the staff are telling him how much they miss him. I laugh and tell her to tell him that I miss him too.

We chat about the guys I have met so far and their lack of suitability since our aim is to "retire young and get diplomatic passports". However, all of the "possibles" seem to possess a quality that takes them out of the running: too short, chews with his mouth open, drinks too much, poor dresser, boring, parties too much...the list is endless. I prepare for work while Karina and I text and send voice notes back and forth. Our conversation continues all the way to breakfast and on my morning commute. When I reach the office, we wish each other a great day and night and end our conversation. It was so refreshing having a good ole girls' chat.

Noah comes around at lunch time to ask whether or not I was interested in joining him and Htet Htet on their quest for noodles. I decline and go to the French bakery instead. Htun Htun and Than Tun have training again today. Htun Htun is so sweet; he says I can still email him if I need him. I smile and tell him that I will be okay. Than Tun is very perceptive. He says that I do not seem well today and he is right. I am not feeling the best; it is a combination of my stomach issue and feeling tired, but I am glad my food stayed down. I told him that my stomach still has not settled. He asked what I ate last night and I tell him about the food but not the drinks.

The CEO comes over and makes me smile when, upon seeing the pile of food on my desk, he asks if they are bringing me food like Buddha. All types of treats are there, including cakes and sweet and savoury pastries. I tell him it is Mima and that he is welcome to some and he accepts the offer. After the CEO leaves, an email pops up and I read it. The email outlines an issue with an old lady who is preventing our contractors from working because she wants more money. A picture of the old lady is attached to the email. She is barely 5 feet tall, not quite 100 pounds and looks like she could be close to 90 years of age. I laugh. Imagine some big strapping men afraid of a tiny old lady.

YANGON SAILING CLUB

Friday, June 27, 2014

As I step out of the elevator this morning, I notice that everyone I encounter is in a jubilant mood; they are all cheerful and chatty and making jokes with each other. I have never seen anything like it. There is euphoria and joy like I have never seen. When I ask what is going on, Than Tun explains to me that it is pay day.

Finance gets help carrying about four large garbage bags on a trolley to the lunchroom. The Myanmar nationals all line up, sign their names and receive an envelope with their cash in it. Since the banking system is not properly developed, most nationals still do not use banks or have a bank account. Khing Sa tells Adam that it is a good day because it is pay day. Khing Sa really is a quiet one who generally does not chat too much in the office, so I am happy to see him finally chatting with Adam.

It is Friday evening and the prospect of the weekend is exciting enough, but, in addition to that, today the CEO invited Adam, Su, Noah and me to the Yangon Sailing Club. I was told that the Club, which was established in 1924, is located by Inya Lake and is a members-only club, except on Fridays when it is open to the public.

At the club, we meet the CEO's wife. She is petite with dark brown hair and a very friendly and outgoing personality. This is also the first time I get to speak to Su properly as she sits next to me in the outdoor seating area. Adam and Noah are sitting near to the CEO and carrying on their conversation with him. Su asks me if I am single and I tell her yes. She tells me she is a single mother with two girls ages six and three. I am surprised because I had assumed she was married. She shows me pictures of the girls and they are beautiful. I want to ask her where the children's father is but perhaps another time; this environment doesn't seem like the best place or time to ask such probing questions. The CEO's wife had earlier suggested that we take up golf as she and her husband are avid players. She says that when we eventually get married it is an activity that we can do with our husbands. Su and I make a plan that we will go and play golf next weekend, so we will get to chat some more. She thinks Adam is "agay" for Noah. When I ask her what she means she tells me that she thinks Adam is gay and in a relationship with Noah. I had just assumed that they were good mates so the thought had never entered my mind, but I suppose I could see how she could come to that assumption.

Adam, Noah and I leave the sailing club at around 7:30 p.m. and Su drops us off at the karaoke bar close to our hotel. I decide to sing Bob Marley's "No Woman, No Cry" and we are in fits of laughter. Let's just say I wouldn't quit my day job to take up singing.

EYEBROW WAXING
— WISH ME LUCK

Saturday, June 28, 2014

After work I take a taxi to Shangri-La Hotel to get my eyebrows waxed. The situation makes me nervous. I don't wear lots of makeup; in fact, I only wear MAC powder plus foundation and lipstick some days, so getting my eyebrows waxed is important.

As I walk into the hotel, I remember the time when I got my eyebrows waxed in Trinidad at a hairdresser on Eastern Main Road. She took out a whole piece of my eyebrow and I had to go straight to Trincity Mall to buy an eyebrow pencil and draw it back in. After that mishap, I am very wary every time I have to try someone new for eyebrow waxing. The taxi driver wants to wait for me, but I tell him not to as I am not sure how long I will be here. The concierge directs me to where the spa is located and I am greeted by a tiny Asian lady whose English is pretty good. She crosses off my name in her appointment book and I am asked to remove my heels and given a pair of white spa slippers. She then goes over to a small table and pours me a tiny cup (with no handles) of warm lemon tea. There is tranquil, relaxing music playing, like you would hear in a yoga or meditation video. After I have finished the tea, she takes me to a small room where I am asked to lie back on the spa table. She asks how I would like them done and I ask her to follow the natural line of my brows and that I normally have the top and bottom waxed along with any stray hairs in the middle. She heats the wax and cleanses both eyebrow areas. She then tests the heat of the wax at the back of her hands, places it on my brows and covers the wax with a tiny cotton strip. Then, with one swift movement, she removes the strip. The process is repeated on my right eyebrow. She then takes a tweezer and plucks any stray hairs not caught by the wax then applies a wax cleanser to clean away any residual wax. She is very precise. I look in the mirror and I am pleased with the result. No need to rush out and buy a pencil this time.

MANICURES AND PEDICURES

Sunday, June 29, 2014

After a successful eyebrow waxing, my fears have been allayed and I decide to take Ava and Jennifer's advice and try the nail salon close to work. I am less scared than the eyebrow waxing as manicures and pedicures can be easily fixed if something goes wrong. I call to make the appointment for today and I specify that I want an express pedicure for my toes and a gel manicure for my nails.

When I arrive at the nail salon for my scheduled appointment, I am seated next to an expat lady and she strikes up a conversation, introducing herself as Selena. As we chat, she disclosed that she used to work for the company I am with but now works for another company here in Yangon. Selena is also in the nail salon for a mani-pedi combo and, as the technicians work on our nails, she teaches them to pronounce my name. Selena has been in Yangon longer than I have and she tells me all the cool spots to get my hair blow-dried and eyebrows waxed. Her hair seems to be in perfect condition. It looks as though it has been recently blow-dried and trimmed and she is wearing it in a bob just above her shoulders. Before she leaves, Selena invites me to catch up with coffee later this week and we exchange numbers.

I decide to choose red nail polish for both my fingernails and toenails. Red has always been my go-to colour for lipstick and nail polish. The service provided by the girls is amazing. They are attentive and efficient and even make the effort to engage in a little chit-chat in the little English they speak as they work on my nails. I would definitely return. They charge K14,500 in total and I can't believe how inexpensive it is.

I gather my things and five minutes later I am on the sidewalk hailing a taxi back to hotel. As it is Sunday, I don't plan to do anything else except relax. While flicking between fashion TV, a local Myanmar channel and HBO, I get a text from Noah telling me not to come downstairs at the hotel because the guys are out of control. That's fine with me because I had no real intention of going back down. I strip myself of my street clothes, exchange them for comfortable cotton shorts and a T-shirt and then settle in my room for a bit before I have to consider what I will have for lunch.

I am half watching a CNN special on the illegal kidney trade in Nepal when my phone alerts me to a new WhatsApp message. It is Kwame whom I met a few days ago after an offsite meeting and had totally forgotten about. Kwame, who is an IT consultant, is Nigerian but has lived in Slovakia and now lives in Melbourne. In the message, he is telling me he had a crazy week in Yangon and flew out to Singapore on Thursday. He just arrived in Bandung, Indonesia an hour ago and will be heading back to Melbourne on Wednesday. I met so many people that day that I had totally forgotten the brief encounter I had with Kwame and that we had exchanged numbers to catch up for a coffee. The text said that he will be back in Yangon around the middle of July and he will give me a call to see what I am up to.

"SA PYI BI LA?" — HAVE YOU FINISHED YOUR LUNCH?

Monday, June 30, 2014

I have now spent a full month here and this is the beginning of my fifth week. I actually ate Asian food today for lunch and not just because it was raining and I couldn't get to the French bakery; it was by choice. I had the sweet and sour chicken with white rice. It was fine. Yangon continues to grow on me with each passing day. Even my stomach seems to be more accepting of Asian food.

Tou Za who works in the Finance Department called me by name and asked if I had finished my lunch. I was so surprised that she actually knew my name. "Have you finished your lunch?" is the standard greeting in Myanmar. It is the equivalent of "How are you?". Food is such an important aspect of Burmese culture that it is reflected in the language. The entire office is a mad scramble today as it is the board meeting tomorrow and each department has to provide slides with updates on their progress to be included in the presentation to the board. Sean is coming to Yangon from Ireland to attend the board meeting so I am excited about that. The last time I saw him was in

London on the journey over here as I had to give him some important files. We will no doubt have lots of catching up to do on what has been happening in the Caribbean.

Thursday, July 3, 2014

I haven't had a chance to write for the last few days. I don't know why; I haven't been inordinately busy or stressed or anything. I have so much to tell that I am not sure where to begin. The board meeting was Tuesday evening. Sean was here and we all went out to dinner. He is really hilarious and we always have a great time. It was good to catch up on what's happening on the other side of the world.

I had to attend a meeting today where I got to meet Svein who works for another company. He is in his thirties and Norwegian. I have never met anyone from Norway before. Despite his young age he holds a very senior position in the company. I wonder what his story is. I need to find out more information about him, but I am not sure who to ask. I tell Keisha about him and she goes to check him out on LinkedIn. She says that I have a type, but I don't agree with her.

GIRLS' NIGHT OUT

Friday, July 4, 2014

I get a message from Ben saying that he hopes my hotel is comfortable and he heard that there is a nine-to-five curfew in Myanmar. There is a curfew, but it is not in Yangon where I am. It is in Mandalay which is 300 miles away and Myanmar's second largest city. Authorities imposed the curfew in Mandalay late Thursday after attacks on minority Muslims left two people dead and 14 injured, raising fears that the ethnic violence that has plagued the country for two years may escalate again.

The unrest started on Tuesday night. I was probably too busy when we were all out to dinner to pay attention to the news. Apparently, there were rumours that a Muslim tea shop owner raped a Buddhist girl. Authorities deployed hundreds of police on Tuesday after a crowd of more than 300 Buddhists marched to the tea shop singing the national anthem. According to news reports, police fired rubber bullets to try to disperse the crowd but failed to control groups that scattered into the streets throwing stones at a mosque and causing minor damage to its exterior, while others ransacked Muslim-owned shops. Several cars were set on fire or had windows shattered by stones and bricks. Muslims account for about four per cent of Myanmar's roughly 60 million people. Myanmar, a predominantly Buddhist nation, has been grappling with violence since 2012 which has left up to 280 people dead and 140,000 others homeless, most of them Muslims attacked by Buddhist militants. Most of the unrest has taken place in the western Rakhine State.

As I sit at my desk working, I glance up to see Noah calmly walking towards me carrying his laptop bag and a plastic bag. When he gets closer, he tells me that he has been relieved of his duties. It is 5 p.m. so I think maybe he is getting an early evening, but he repeats himself and then adds plainly that he has been fired. I don't think he is serious as I know he likes to joke around, so I ask him again and he confirms it. I don't even know what to make of it. I am absolutely stunned. Without saying anything else he turns and walks in the direction of the exit.

After Noah leaves, I sit there in a daze for a while. Noah fired? What happened? Elliot comes to me and asks me if I have heard and if I know the reason. I say I am not sure, but I know that the CEO was looking for him this morning for some numbers and no one could find him. I speculate that that may have had something to do with it. A few moments later, Adam comes to me and says that we should have a chat. We go to one of the offices and he says I must have heard by now. I share with him what I thought and what I heard. He seems really shaken up and upset about the entire thing. I am emotionless about these things. As far as I am concerned it is just business and I feel that Noah may have brought some of his predicament on himself. Adam explained to me that he stuck his neck out to get Noah's contract extended and he felt that Noah should at least have had the chance to speak to his team. I am neither here nor there about it. I think it was best handled as it was. I tell him it is just business and not to worry too much or be too broken up about it. You simply have to be strong in these things.

He understands that Noah may be at Union and he says if I see Noah I should tell him that he feels really bad about the entire thing.

* * *

The long-awaited ladies' night is tonight. A ladies' night was Ava's idea. For weeks she had been trying to organise it, but one thing or other kept popping up, which ended up clashing with our plans and causing persons to have to reschedule. Ava, Helen who is a Filipino from the site acquisition team, Su, Jennifer and I are going to dinner at Manhattan Fish Market and later to Union Bar. We have set the time for 7:30 p.m. Instead of going straight there from the office, I decide that I will go back to the hotel to change bags and relieve myself of my laptop before catching up with the girls later. Finn is leaving at the same time and we share a cab back to the hotel. Sean is right — he is pleasant enough. During the cab ride we talk about our respective weeks, our time with the company and the relocation process. I learn that Finn is gay, or, as Su would say, "agay", and his partner is here in Yangon with him. I think to myself, *There you go, Sean. He is gay.* One prospect has been removed from the running. That would explain why he doesn't hang out much with the others. I totally understand as well since the other guys are all testosterone walking on legs and I doubt they would be able to relate. They may also give him a hard time. I resolve at that moment that we will become friends.

When we reach the hotel, we are greeted by the posse which includes Noah, Evan and Katherine. I say goodbye to Finn and go up in the elevator to put down my things and change bags. I try to charge both my phones as both batteries are very low. When I head back down, I stop briefly by the outdoor terrace where the others are seated and tell the group that I won't be staying long as I am going to ladies' night. I sit briefly and realise they are discussing Noah's plans now that he has been relieved of his duties. I vaguely remember Katherine telling a story about a card they gave someone at her previous job that read, "Congrats on getting out". I am not really enthusiastic about being a part of the conversation about Noah, so I tell them that I am starving, which is the truth, and I leave to meet the girls.

When I arrive at the Manhattan Fish Market it is not at all as I expected. Silly me, I was expecting an actual fish market, but it was a very modern restaurant. It seems like I am the first of the group to arrive. The host/waiter asks how many persons and, since I am not sure who exactly is coming this evening, I say five. I know it will be Ava and Helen for sure and Su had sent a text to say she will be late. The host/waiter guides me over to a six-seater table near the middle of the room. I take a quick glance at the menu and I order the calamari and a tonic water immediately. As I sit down, I realise my local phone has died and, using my Barbados phone, I send a WhatsApp and Skype message to Ava to let her know I am here and that she could let the others know. I try to get the local phone on so that I can text Su but it is really dead, so I hope that she texts Helen if she tries to reach me and I don't respond.

When they finally arrive, I am halfway through my calamari. I offer them some and the waiter comes back to take our orders. I have the most amazing Mediterranean butter fish with rice and vegetables. A month ago I would not have had the fish, but now I just eat and hope for the best. Helen has the pasta and Ava has fried mushrooms and fish and chips. During dinner I learn that Helen, who is from the Philippines, is married with two kids and her husband is visiting for the weekend. He will arrive at 3 a.m. on Saturday. We tease her that she will be getting a booty call. We chat about our favourite vacation spots and Ava shares her dating stories and experiences in Myanmar since she has been here the longest of all of us and is leaving shortly to take up another position in PNG. She says that the dating scene in Yangon is not very easy since people tend to talk about each other a lot. The way she describes it, it seems all very high-schoolish to me. When she learns that I met her former colleague Selena, she mentions that she and Selena had a very bad falling out. She does not go into details and I am not sure I want to know anyway.

Su finally arrives and tells us she is late because she had to take her daughter to the doctor. Thankfully, the doctor said that she is fine. As the night goes on, I learn that Ava is 31 while Su is 35 with two kids and married but currently separated. Helen is 38. The four of us are all in our thirties, from various parts of the world but work and sisterhood have brought us together. Ellen and Su tell me that they thought I was 25 when they first met me. I smile and thank them. I certainly don't feel 25. Su explains to us that all the going out and drinking is very new for her and even though she is a grown woman her mother still worries very much about her. She has only been separated from her husband for six months, but she doesn't think that she would date an expat. Jennifer comes and joins us just as we are having dessert. She doesn't stay very long and gives a very vague excuse about having something to do (*Is she a member of the mafia? Who has something to do at this hour?* I think), but she will catch up later.

When we have had our fill of conversation and food, we go next door to Union. Germany is playing France in a quarter-final match of World Cup football and the place is packed. We meet Antonio, an Italian from Sicily who is opening a pizza place in Yangon. He jokes that we should watch the movie *The Sicilian*. He hears I am from Barbados and tells me he used to live in Bermuda. I smoke some cigarettes that Helen gives me and drink some wine. I am having a great time at our ladies' night and I think it would be a good idea if we try to do it once a month.

SHAN YOE YAR AND GREEN ELEPHANT

Saturday, July 5, 2014

I go to work in the morning and in the afternoon I meet Logan's friends, Mark and Lucia, for lunch. Mark is from Holland and Lucia is from Slovakia. They seem quite laidback and chill and I am happy to hang out with people who are not connected to work.

Mark and Lucia explain to me that they met Logan randomly on a diving trip in the Middle East a couple years ago and had stayed in touch. Apparently, when he found out that I was leaving on a secondment to Yangon he told them I was going to be here the same time that they would be and that we should connect. I don't remember Logan telling me any of this, however, I am pleased that they took the time to reach out and to meet up with me.

They are both volunteering in Yangon with Care, an organisation that empowers women by equipping them with a number of skills, including computer skills and English literacy. We have lunch at a restaurant called Shan Yoe Yar. The restaurant is housed in a century-old traditional teak house with rattan chairs with maroon-coloured cushions. It has been renovated in the style of the Shan Haw Palaces with the modern touch of air conditioning. This is the first restaurant I have been to which serves Myanmar food. The food is from the Shan State which borders China to the north, Laos to the east, Thailand to the south and five administrative divisions of Myanmar in the west. I let them order since they are more familiar with Myanmar dishes. Shan food is cooked over wood or charcoal fire which makes it different from other Burmese cuisine. I was also told it is less oily. They order a selection of dishes to share as this is how the food is intended to be eaten. The dishes include green mango salad, an eggplant curry dish, seafood balls on lemon grass skewers, a spicy crispy chicken dish, banana leaf pounded fish (fish in a banana leaf), potato cakes, deep-fried tamarind sea bass with ginger and peanuts, sour pickled vegetables and a fried rice dish. The sea bass is orgasmic. We talk about our respective jobs, the possibility of them visiting Logan in the Caribbean and their impressions of Myanmar. The food is absolutely amazing, a taste sensation with lots of spices and herbs, and I am glad that I was brave and decided to try it. I will definitely be back to this restaurant.

In the evening, I finally meet Finn's partner Johnathan who is a doctor from the South Pacific. The five of us — Ava, Adam, Finn, Johnathan and I — have dinner at the Green Elephant. The Green Elephant is an Asian restaurant serving Chinese, Thai, Burmese and Western dishes located in an old two-storey wooden house. We are escorted upstairs to a private dining room with green placemats and green plates and various elephant paintings and elephant wood carvings around the room. The food is underwhelming compared to the delicious Shan food I had at lunchtime, but the company more than makes up for it. Johnathan has cropped gel-styled dark hair, and is wearing a white linen shirt and khaki pants as though he just stepped off the cover of a GQ magazine. He is initially quiet, but when we start to ask him questions we can tell that he is very intelligent and engaging. We learn that he is of Rotuman ethnicity and he shares with us his experiences working in the ER in Fiji. He does not practice anymore but is more into public health administration now and has done a lot of work with persons living with HIV. I am very impressed by his work and tell him about the UWI HARP Programme for children infected with and affected by HIV that I volunteered with in Barbados during my university days. I can see that Johnathan, Finn and I will become fast friends.

SELF-CARE SUNDAY

Sunday, July 6, 2014

I wake up earlier than I normally do for a Sunday. I had already sorted the laundry on Saturday night, so I just take it downstairs to the front desk for the laundry service. I chat with my best friend Keisha for a bit on Blackberry messenger. She tells me that she has been spending time with Nic and I am happy that they are finding solace in each other now that I am away.

Keisha and I have been good friends since we were about sixteen, but knew each other from the time we were eleven, and Nicole and I met when we were both studying law at university. I go down to breakfast after my chat with Keisha and the breakfast area is largely empty. I see the South African and I am relieved that he does not come over. I am not in the mood to have polite conversation with him.

I have decided that I will take a trip to Singapore since there is a long weekend coming up in Yangon. It will be a chance to have a break from Yangon and from work colleagues who I am surrounded by at work and at the hotel and then again on weekends when we hang out. It is as though work and free time have merged into one for me. Back in my room, I check out the hotel rates and look at pictures of the hotel rooms for Singapore. I then send an email to Khin Marla to remind her to contact the agent regarding my flights. I hope she understands what I want. Because the Burmese are not natural English speakers, they sometimes do not readily understand what is being said.

Adam sends a text that he is going to have lunch with Noah around 12:30 and asks if I am keen. I respond by saying that I have a few things to do and won't be able to make it. Truth is, I don't feel like hanging out with anyone and would rather some time to myself. I am about to wash my hair and that is a task in and of itself. I know there is absolutely no way that I will finish washing and drying my hair by 12:30 and I don't feel like rushing it either, so I decline. Sometimes you have to prioritise yourself. I do some research online and see that there is an ethnic hair salon in Singapore. I am slightly overjoyed and I take down the number and the address. I read a review that the salon is a little expensive, but I may have to make an appointment to go there nevertheless. I will pay them whatever they want. My personal commandment No.11 is: "Thou cannot walk around with 'pop down' hair", but I am scared that I may end up with no hair if it all goes horribly wrong. I may still chance it, knowing that I have eight more weeks left in Yangon and at least the hairdresser speaks English and should understand what I want done with my hair. I will try to make an appointment later in the week. It is amazing the things we take for granted in Barbados where there are hairdressers in abundance who know just how to manage curly hair.

I don't do much for the rest of the day except relax and surf online which takes what seems like a year since the internet is extremely slow. I watch Al Jazeera while I am surfing. Al Jazeera is a news network based in Qatar which covers news from all over the globe and is not as biased as the American news channels and tends to offer a more balanced perspective on world events. The situation with Isis in Iraq is the main news. Argentina, Brazil, Germany and Holland are now in the semi-finals of the World Cup. The laundry service returns my laundry close to evening time and I remember that we are to take head shot pictures tomorrow at work, so I give the skinny young boy a long-sleeved white shirt to iron for me.

I do not even leave the hotel room for dinner but order room service instead. I work on a presentation which is slated for Wednesday but the slides are due tomorrow. I am actually pleased when I complete the presentation as it takes longer than I thought it would and I would have been pissed with myself if I had waited to do it on Monday.

When I wake up from my evening nap outside is dark. I decide to spend some time doing a little packing for my Singapore trip. I wish that Keisha was here to help me pack for this trip as well, but since she isn't, I know this process will take me a while. After that, I focus on fixing my hair and getting ready for the week ahead. With the assistance of the mirror mounted on the medicine cabinet door in the bathroom, I part my hair and install two perfect French braids and I use a black elastic band to hold them together at the nape of my neck.

Since I have been to Yangon I have been busy exploring and socialising with my friends and colleagues and I haven't really been able to enjoy days like this one. It feels good to pause for a little me time. When you look after yourself, you are saying to yourself: I am on my side! I see a WhatsApp message from Sean and during our text conversation I tell him that I will be going to Singapore. He thinks that the break from Yangon will be good. I send a message to Lynette who is Singaporean and whom I met at the hotel restaurant a month ago as I was finishing up my Saturday breakfast. Lynette works for an international children's charity, so I send the message to see if she is in Yangon or Singapore and to tell her when I will be in Singapore in case she wants to meet up. I eventually turn off the lights and sign off around midnight even though I do not feel tired.

MONDAY MORNING BLUES

Monday, July 7, 2014

The alarm goes off at 6:15 a.m. and I let it snooze for five minutes. I am now halfway through my stint in Yangon. Six weeks, to be exact. As I begin to prepare for work this morning, I am acutely conscious of this and I am reminded once again that I will soon have to finalise my decision on whether I will extend my time in Yangon or go home at the end of the three months.

I get up and call the front desk and ask them to send my shirt. However, as I am going to the bathroom, I hear a knock on the door and I am surprised when I open it to see a gentleman from housekeeping standing there with an iron and ironing board. It takes me five minutes to explain that I do not want an iron and ironing board. It is hilarious. I try to explain that I sent a shirt to be ironed yesterday evening which I want to wear this morning but haven't got it back. At first, he thinks I am asking for my laundry and tries to explain that the laundry service is not a 24-hour service. I explain it is one shirt that needed to be ironed. I tell him I am going to shower and ask him to bring back the ironed shirt to my room. He finally understands and leaves. I barely step out of the shower before I hear another knock on the door and I am relieved to see the lad with my shirt. I thank him and tip him, which he initially doesn't want to accept as tipping is not expected. However, he graciously accepts the tip and I slip back into my room to get dressed and then head down to breakfast.

The breakfast area is packed and noisy. I scan the room for an empty seat and I spot Finn and go to sit with him. Adam arrives just after me and joins us. As we busy ourselves with eating breakfast, the guys engage in some small talk. Finn says that he visited the Myanmar Coffee House yesterday while Adam went to play basketball with the Filipinos. I imagine Adam playing with the Filipinos and I chuckle; Adam is over 6 feet and the Filipinos are barely five feet tall. He must have felt like Shaq playing with them.

We leave and Chok, the driver, is outside waiting for us. As we make our usual morning commute, Adam asks if the reason I did not join them yesterday was because I had to run errands, but I tell him I was just really tired and needed to rest. Adam talks about his lunch with Noah and Evan yesterday and I am sort of glad that I didn't go since Evan was there until Adam says that Noah left Yangon last night. I am disappointed that he left without saying goodbye and I am slightly saddened that I didn't make an effort to go and have lunch with them. However, how was I to know he was leaving so soon and that would have been his last day in Yangon? Sigh.

In spite of all the rest I had yesterday I still have Monday morning blues. Than Tun senses that something is wrong and tells me that I do not seem well today. I tell him that I have a migraine.

FOLDED BILLS AND GOVERNMENT OFFICES

Tuesday, July 8, 2014

There is a bell that looks like an old school bell that hangs from a metal contraption in the office. Every time a communications tower is successfully constructed someone dangles the rope and rings the bell to let us know we have successfully completed another tower. The first time it rang I was a bit startled, but then Than Tun explained what it was all about.

The bell was rung again today after being silent for some days now. The staff all clap and cheer and let out loud whistles. Every time the bell rings it means we are getting closer to getting Myanmar connected and I am excited about that. I am also excited that I am going to Singapore on Friday and I am considering going to the hairdresser there.

My ticket arrives around 2 p.m. by courier and I am relieved that the agent got the flights and my name correct. I, of course, have to pay for the ticket in cash which amounts to US$403 for a three-hour return flight to Singapore. The agent refuses to accept my folded US$100 bill just like the young lady at the hotel's reception desk did when I had first come to Yangon. What is it with not accepting folded US bills?

I will have to get rid of it in Singapore. I make my appointment at the hairdresser in Singapore and she says that she does not accept credit cards so it will cost about 150 Singapore dollars (SG$). I make the appointment for 6 p.m. as my flight is expected to arrive in Singapore at 3:10 p.m., if all goes well.

We have some leases to register and to say that it has been a royal headache would be an understatement. It seems as though we are always playing a game of cat and mouse with the officers at the registrar. It was explained that it is hard to catch the officers in the morning. They arrive around 10:30 a.m. and then they go for a tea break for about one hour, so that takes them to about 11:30 a.m. Then they go to lunch at 12 p.m. So, in reality, they don't start any work until 2 p.m. and then they close at 3 p.m. so that they can review all the documents and close all the cases for the day. However, if you pay them extra, they will open the office for about five or six hours for you and they will even open for you on a Sunday.

SOME SMART COOKIES

Wednesday, July 9, 2014

I facilitated the legal module today for the management development programme. It is days like this that make me want to stay in Yangon forever. Ten locals from various business units have been earmarked for management positions. They are a brilliant bunch and I love them all. Than Tun is the cheekiest of the group and keeps you on your toes. He is definitely the kind of student you want in your class. When I was going through the challenges that the company faces, he reminded me to consider the religious challenge since the country is largely Buddhist.

After the presentation I ask if they have any questions. The girls cheekily ask if I am single. I tell them I am single in Yangon and they all laugh. They want to know my age, so I tell them and they all say I look younger. I thank them for their kindness, bless their hearts. I then ask all of them the same questions, as it is only fair. They all range in ages from 24 to 38. San San, the engineer, is only 24 and this is her first job. I think it is excellent that she gets to be on the management development programme so early in her career as she has lots of potential. She is also the top scorer on the individual quiz that I give. Some of the girls say they are single and want to get married eventually, but they lament the suitability of candidates. I tell them I can totally relate. It seems to be the case all over.

I like that it is really easy to change your manicure colours in Yangon. It costs K13,000 (US$13) for them to take off my old gel polish, apply a new coat of polish and change the colour on my toes as well. When I enter the spa there is another woman of colour sitting on one of the pedicure chairs. She is wearing her hair in the locs hairstyle. I spot her easily as she looks like a plump Oprah with dreadlocks and we are the only black people in the entire spa. My nail tech seats me in the chair beside her as it is the only vacant chair and we smile and greet each other. She introduces herself as Yvonne and notes that I am the only other black woman she has seen since she came to Yangon a few months ago. I know exactly what she means; Black women are scarce in these parts. As we chat, I learn that Yvonne is from the UK but has family in Jamaica. She is an international entrepreneurship consultant and has worked in Europe and Africa. When I tell her what I do and where I am working, she says she is familiar with the company that I am working for. She tells me about her experience in Yangon and how people are always staring at her. Sometimes when she goes to the supermarket a group of people would come into her aisle just to stare at her. They would come so close to her sometimes that they invade her space.

I explain to her that when I first got here the locals used to stare a lot as well. I am not sure if they have stopped staring as much or if I have stopped noticing. I tell her that when I went to Dala the rickshaw driver told me that I should wear *thanaka* on my face, that I could blend in that way. Thanaka is a yellowish-white cosmetic paste made from ground tree bark which is applied to the face by Burmese women. It is meant to protect the skin from sunburn and prevent it from premature ageing. I, however, still have not tried it. Yvonne and I share a laugh as I recount my experience in Dala. Her laugh is lively and infectious. She says that she doesn't think that she would have had a similar experience in Dala — I am petite and "dainty" with pretty pecan brown skin while her complexion is more espresso brown and she has a thick body structure. Yvonne is very animated and I am so happy that we have this chance encounter. When she is about to leave, she tells me she is living near the British Embassy near the Strand Hotel, and she leaves me her card. I am sorry to see her go, but I promise to give her a call.

The girls finish my nails and toes and realise that I only have my peep toe heels. They won't let me put them on and say that my toes will take at least an hour to dry. I am not prepared to spend another hour in the nail salon waiting for my nails to dry so I give one of the girls K5,000 and she runs out to buy me some thongs and returns with a pair for about K3,000. I pay them for their services and give them a generous tip. They were so great with me.

When I get back to the hotel, I see Evan, whom I have not seen in a while, sitting alone, so I go and chat with him for a bit and smoke a cigarette. Evan is moving out of the hotel and into Ava's old apartment as Ava is leaving Yangon shortly to take up a regional position at the company's PNG office. Adam later joins us. I chat with them for a bit longer about the construction challenges Evan has been having with the monsoon weather and then I go upstairs to shower.

SINGAPORE TRAVEL PLANS SCUPPERED

Thursday, July 10, 2014

One more day till Singapore. I am anxious, however, that I only have three pages left in my passport. I have Keisha contact the embassy in Barbados and they say that the nearest consulate that may be able to help me is in London. I think that is unfortunate. If I fly to London I may as well do the other leg to Barbados. I am considering staying in Yangon longer and so the dwindling pages is a concern, especially since some places like Thailand need a full page for a visa.

The bell rang again today.

While we are all at our desks working, the South African brings his phone to Than Tun and asks him to speak to the contractor from the site he visited yesterday. However, Than Tun shakes his head to say that he did not visit a site yesterday so it could not have been him. Despite this, the South African extends the phone to Than Tun again, gesturing for him to take it. I am about to intervene to confirm that it couldn't have been Than Tun because he was on the management development programme yesterday when Win Tin jumps up and says it was him. Apparently, the neighbours are threatening the contractors and they are afraid. Win Tin advises that they should continue working as they are only verbal threats. If they come with sticks, the contractors should go and complain to the township council. The South African's interpretation is hilarious. He says in his strong Afrikaans accent, "If they bring a stick, stop work and run away."

Su is wearing the traditional dress today because there was another office photoshoot. This is the first time I am seeing her in traditional dress. It looks like an expensive one. The dress is a lovely green and black and consists of a luxurious round-necked silk short-sleeved top which stops at waist level. The skirt (or longyi) portion of the dress is ankle length and has an intricate zigzag pattern. She is really beautiful. She calls Than Tun away from his desk and he readily goes. I cannot tell what the discussion is about.

Today is the last day of the work week as it is a public holiday tomorrow and I wait for Khin Marla who works in HR and is responsible for travel documentation to send my documents to get back into Myanmar when I travel to Singapore. If she had sent those documents ages ago, I wouldn't have to be enduring the wait now. I finally get them close to 6 p.m. She had to send them to Mima through Skype so that I could get them. She sends a text to apologise for the inconvenience caused, but I am just grateful that they have finally arrived. I take the documents to Ava and ask her one last time if I would have an issue getting back into Myanmar. Initially she says that I wouldn't, but then she asks what type of visa I have and when I tell her she thinks that I may have a challenge returning after all. She calls Khin Marla to check and she confirms that I will have an issue gaining entry into Myanmar since I have a Barbados passport which is not among the list of passports that benefit from special entry exemptions. To get back into Myanmar, I would need to travel to Malaysia or Thailand to get another visa. Because of this, I have to cancel my Singapore trip at the last moment. I am disappointed as I had my hopes set on visiting Singapore to get away and try the food and shops and get my hair done. But it wouldn't have made sense me going if I couldn't get back into Myanmar. Adam suggests I go to Bagan instead but, even though I had made a mental note many weeks ago to visit Bagan before I left Myanmar, I ignore his suggestion. I do not want to think about how frustrating it would be to try to arrange a hotel and flight again, especially on such short notice.

CHINATOWN IN MYANMAR

Friday, July 11, 2014

When I wake up, I cannot help but think that I was supposed to be in Singapore today. I call the salon to let them know that I need to cancel my appointment since my travel plans have changed. The lady on the other end is very understanding. I do not get out of bed. I miss breakfast. I do not feel like doing anything as the disappointment of not being able to experience Singapore is still very fresh. Sean suggests I go to KL or Bangkok and I would have considered going if only booking flights and hotels from Myanmar were that easy.

I eventually get up, shower and go down to lunch. I see Johnathan, Finn's partner, in the hotel restaurant a few tables away from me, but I just wave to him and he waves back. I don't go over to chat as he is busy typing away on his laptop. When I finish my lunch, however, I pass by his table for a quick chat. He greets me warmly and tells me that he is preparing for an international conference on AIDS which is being held in Melbourne next week where he will be delivering a paper. We chat for a bit about my quashed travel plans and the lack of housing options in Myanmar. He says he would have the same visa headache regarding re-entering Myanmar since he has a Fijian passport. I eventually bid him goodbye and head back upstairs.

I lie down and close my eyes to think. If I leave Myanmar on a weekend trip, getting back in seems to be an issue, so I will have to be content to explore other parts of the country despite the travel restrictions in some areas. Oh, the headache of booking a flight to Bagan now so late in the day! I am not in the mood to stress myself out. I decide that I will go to Bagan another weekend. I fall asleep again and when I wake up it is close to 3 p.m. Housekeeping comes to clean my room and I decide that instead of moping inside the hotel all day I will check out 19th Street Yangon — the city's Chinatown. I make a little extra effort selecting what I will wear to help lift my mood. I decide on a simple, 100% cotton, light yellow Broderie Anglaise dress with patch pockets and an A-line silhouette and my nude ballet flats. It is the type of dress I imagine you would wear when you let your hair down and happily dance through sunflower fields. Wearing it had made me feel happy in the past and it was a gift from my Auntie Ann. I jump into the taxi downstairs and I tell the driver where I am going. He charges me K4,000 for the fifteen minute ride to 19th Street.

Chinatown is an authentic Myanmar experience. People in market stalls are selling everything and anything. Some people have set up their goods on low tables outside the shop fronts, while others have them spread out on cloths on the ground. There are lots of brightly coloured umbrellas and low plastic stools. There is raw meat of every type — pork, prawns, fish, whole chicken with head and feet included — vegetables, herbs, pineapples, mangoes and durian being sold. Some of the smells are not pleasant. Other stalls are selling street food. These include fried insects, satay, snack rotis, fried prawn cake, corn cake, dosa (Indian crepes), fried dough and sugar and Myanmar BBQ (basically any type of kebab you could think of). The narrow 19th Street reminds me of the Tunapuna Market in Trinidad — that sort of lively, noisy, vibrant, bustling, grimy vibe — except that everyone is Asian. As I walk along the street slowly and soak in the atmosphere, I see a lady standing in front of one the shops burning fake money in a large metal bucket to send to her deceased Chinese ancestors. The hungry orange flame in the bucket is going and she keeps adding stacks of fake bills to the fire as she recites prayers under her breath. I pause briefly directly in front of her to watch her actions, careful not to let my jaw touch the ground in awe, but the locals carry on with their business and I gather they must be used to this. When I feel I have paused long enough, I continue further up the street and see a line of monks passing through in their maroon-coloured robes. Further along, I see a few tourists sitting on low plastic chairs and drinking Myanmar beer outside one of the shops. It is very hot and sticky outside and I am glad I chose the light cotton dress as I would have been stewing in any other attire. The streets are very narrow and I have to mind how I go as cars are allowed to drive through the already crowded streets. After about two hours of taking in 19th Street, the rain starts to pour. I take it as my cue that it is time to leave as Adam had mentioned to me that from 6 p.m. or so is when all the major barbecuing and partying starts and the street gets even busier. I have certainly had enough of people jostling me, so I try to find a taxi to take me back to the hotel.

As soon as I am in the hotel room Keisha calls. She tells me about some solid waste tax that the government has implemented back in Barbados for homeowners and how her landlady is talking about raising the rent. I am only half listening as I am thinking I may have to go into the office tomorrow.

ADAM IS LEAVING
FOR MELBOURNE

Saturday, July 12, 2014

I feel happy and refreshed after the day off. I get up and shower. Out of courtesy, I send a text to Adam asking him if he needs any help in the office today or with finding things for his new place (he only recently secured a suitable house to rent), but I hope he doesn't need any help with either. When I go down to breakfast, I see Adam talking to one of the girls at the front desk and I slip into the breakfast area hoping that he doesn't see me.

Finn and Johnathan are at breakfast and I say hello and put down my laptop on a table close to theirs. Finn tells me he is not going into the office and I tell him that I am relieved that I am not the only one. Adam joins me at the table soon after and tells me that he is not going into the office either. He explained that he has used up all the credit on his phone so he couldn't respond to my text, but he will let me know if he needs any help with shopping. I would prefer if he doesn't; I would just rather do my own thing today. He suggests a trip to Mandalay for the night, but I can't book a flight if there is no internet. I tell him I am sure that I will find something to do other than go to Mandalay.

He chats a bit and tells me he will be gone for a week from July 25 to August 5. He has to go back to Melbourne to wrap up things, say goodbye to some people and get some growths removed that could be pre-cancerous. I tell him to come back please. Myanmar just wouldn't be the same for me without Adam, but also, I didn't want to have to take up the slack of solely leading our team here in Myanmar and, in so doing, forfeit the option of returning to Barbados and the Caribbean after my three-month stint. Finn and Johnathan leave at this point and I comment on what a cute couple they are as we watch them walk out of the restaurant together. Now that we are alone, I take this opportunity to ask Adam how things are going with his girlfriend and he says they get to chat sometimes via Skype. He thought it would be easy as he felt one of them would hate their job and would want to move to be with the other person, but they both love their jobs. I ask him if she would consider coming here to Yangon, but he doesn't know. He thinks that she may be over Asia as she grew up in Singapore. We chat some more about some dodgy clubs he went to and I laugh and tell him I can take those off my list then.

THE HUNT FOR HAIR RELAXER

Sunday, July 13, 2014

I checked out Taw Win Centre today. It is considered one of the major shopping centres in Yangon and is only a ten-minute drive from my hotel. However, it turned out to be another hodgepodge of stores similar to the Junction Square which I visited last month. I have been desperately searching for some relaxer for my hair and I read that there is a Paul Mitchell store there. I visit the store and I see some of the products I used when I wore my hair curly like the Round Trip curl definer, but there is no relaxer in sight.

I decide not to waste my trip to the Taw Win Centre and I casually begin to check out some of the other stores. It is more crowded than Junction Square but also has a reputation for being budget-friendly so that would explain the crowds. Every other store is a clothing or cosmetics store. I find one solitary skirt in a store and the store attendant tells me it is free size so I am not allowed to try it. I can't imagine that I would wear this skirt anywhere fancy anyway. When I have had my fill of the place, I decide to go to Market Place in search of relaxer or at least some moisturiser. Market Place is a premium supermarket where the expats shop as it carries international brands. It has started to pour now so I ask the taxi driver to wait for me while I run in to investigate their relaxer situation. Based on my search so far for the elusive relaxer in Yangon, I did not have my hopes up, but I find myself sighing loudly and being slightly annoyed when I realise once again that there is no relaxer here either. I race back to the waiting taxi to escape the downpour and, still empty-handed, I ask my taxi driver to drop me off at the hotel. He charges me K6,000 from Taw Win Centre to Market Place and from Market Place to the hotel.

As I am heading to the elevator, I spot Finn in the lobby. He says he is waiting on Johnathan to come downstairs so they can head out for a bit. I chat with Finn a little and we decide on what time we will be going to Ava's goodbye party at Jennifer's place. We make plans to meet in the lobby at 4:45 p.m. Even though I am still not a huge fan of Ava, I want to see Jennifer's place. She is staying at the Shangri-La Residences. I go upstairs, shower and take a nap. When I wake up it is still raining outside and I am shocked to realise that it is already 4:30 p.m. I jump out of my bed and hurriedly prepare myself to meet Finn in the lobby.

* * *

When we get there, Jennifer's place is everything I expected it would be. It is located at one of the most desired addresses in Yangon and we are asked to leave our IDs at the gate before being directed by the security guard to where we should go on the premises. The three-bedroom apartment is an oasis of luxury and calm, with a way better view than the one I have at my hotel. It is well-equipped with modern amenities and it would be hard not to be extremely comfortable here.

SWEEPSTAKES AND
LONG WAITS

Monday, July 14, 2014

Win Tin won the World Cup Sweepstakes and management matched the prize money. He said he stayed up and watched the entire game with his wife right next to him - she wanted him to win the prize money also. The total prize money is K60,000. I am happy for them.

The company needs to submit a new Form 26 with our change of directors, but the forms are not available in soft copy so our agents have to type in this information for us. We were trying to have this completed since yesterday so that the CFO can use it to open a new bank account. When it is finally done, Adam stamps it with the wrong stamp. It is the most hilarious thing ever when I reflect on it. But in the moment that it happens, I am not pleased and I don't think it is funny at all. I will have to take a taxi to our agents' location to get a newly typed up form. Everything takes a bit longer here.

At lunch time, Adam, Elliot and I decide to try a new Indonesian restaurant that has just opened in our building and what a mistake that was. The food takes fifty minutes to come and Elliot is so frustrated that he decides to leave. When it finally arrives, it is nothing to scream about. Fifty minutes of our lives wasted. I can tell we probably won't be back to that restaurant.

PERSPECTIVE IS EVERYTHING

Wednesday, July 16, 2014

Finn and I have breakfast together this morning and he is such a great and genuine person. We make jokes about how the napkins in the restaurant are really scented tissues. He, too, felt like he was in a twilight zone when he first arrived here. He mentions that he is going back to Ireland in two weeks' time for a two-week holiday as he has not had his annual holiday yet. He says that while he is excited about being home, he doesn't know how he is going to readjust to Ireland since everything is so modern there in comparison to Yangon.

I am at work extra early today and grateful for the peace and relative quiet as only a few persons are around. Adam is in Mandalay today. Htun Htun has just arrived at work, early as well, and he asked me how long I will be staying in Yangon. I tell him just three months and then I have to return to my regular job. He seems sad after my response. I wish I could bottle them all up and take them back to Barbados with me. I will miss them the most from this entire experience, especially cheeky Than Tun. He comes in this morning as I am writing this extract and says, "Ah, you are smiling." I don't tell him that the reason I am smiling is because I am writing and thinking about them. That is the effect they have on me.

I put away my notepad since more people are starting to arrive now and ready myself for the day's tasks. I look across the room and notice that Htet Htet is scolding San San about her attire. Their voices are getting louder now and from my limited Burmese and their gestures I decipher that San San has to go and meet the community leader at 3 p.m., but Htet Htet does not think San San is appropriately dressed. She is wearing a t-shirt and a too-short skirt. San San tugs at her skirt, but I think she eventually gives up and agrees with Htet Htet. They are very animated in their discussion. My phone rings and interrupts my observation of their conversation. It is a number I do not have saved in my phone and, when I answer, I am ready to say that they have the wrong number when a voice declares it is Kwame and he is back in Yangon and keen to go to dinner. He is speaking in a very excited voice like he just won the lottery and I can't help but smile. He says he feels like eating Thai food, but I am sceptical as I do not know that there is a great Thai restaurant close to our hotel. Instead I tell him I will think of somewhere and text him. He jokingly says that if he doesn't hear from me by 4 p.m. he will send the police to look for me. I laugh. I eventually text him back and tell him that we will go to Shan Yoe Yar in the Lanmadaw Township. I am looking forward to eating the food at Shan Yoe Yar again since it was so good the last time.

I go for lunch with the gang at a local place in the shopping complex close to the office called Golden Pearl. I have been here before and it is not my favourite place, but some of the others who I usually have lunch with seem to like it. The proprietor of the establishment has crammed as many tables as could possibly fit into the small space. It is always packed with locals and very hot despite the fans that dot the restaurant. An entire meal with rice and green tea can cost under K3,000 (US$3), but the quality of the food is a little questionable. During the meal Elliot asks me if I am staying in Yangon. Staying or leaving seems to be top of mind for many of the expats. I tell him that I am torn. He tells me I should ask for more money, but I explain that money is not really a deciding factor for me. It will come down to the quality of life that I perceive I can have here and career growth.

Later, Sean also asks whether I will stay in Yangon longer than three months. I am a bit tired of persons asking me this question, especially since I have not worked out my thoughts about it yet. However, after discussing it with Sean, the choice is not so difficult anymore and I no longer feel guilty about having to choose one job location over the other. He helps me to put things in perspective and tells me I should keep my eyes on the bigger picture. He says he sees this type of things happen all the time. People go away on secondments and are forgotten about. They are away from the action so miss out on promotions. I thank him for his advice and he admits to a certain fondness and concern as to my welfare. While I have come to love Yangon and its people, I must think in the interest of my career, and so I choose Barbados as it has more to offer me in terms of future skills.

SHAN YOE YAR TAKE TWO

Thursday, July 17, 2014

Last night was dinner with Kwame and some others at Shan Yoe Yar. Less than two weeks before I had visited this gem of local cuisine with Logan's friends Mark and Lucia and I loved the food. I loved it so much that I vowed to return and I am so happy I did. The food was just as good the second time around.

I arrived first because my OCD wanted to choose the table and the wine in peace. The others arrived soon after, followed by Kwame. We were not impressed that he spent about seven minutes in our presence on the phone. We are all busy but not rude enough to have conversations on our phones at the dinner table. I thought the call may have been orchestrated, but I don't say anything. As we passed around the bottle of wine, Kwame declined to pour himself a glass as he doesn't drink. Great news! More wine to go around. We ordered a range of dishes and Kwame explained his palate — he likes fried foods and no vegetables or anything healthy. As the evening unfolded, we learnt more about Kwame, including that he lost his mother and sister and is trying to get his nine-year-old nephew to Melbourne. Melbourne rarely crosses my thoughts except that Adam lived and worked there and lots of people in Myanmar seem to like it.

We were all intrigued by Kwame's Nigerian culture and his experiences in Slovakia and we paid rapt attention as Kwame shared his stories over dinner. Because he is Nigerian and polygamous unions are popular there, we joked about him having three wives, but he doesn't actually have three wives or any wife, for that matter. He told us about his experience with a child in Slovakia who licked him on the train because he thought he was made of chocolate. His job as a consultant takes him all over the world. He also thought it fit to share that the Nordic women are more open-minded about sex than any of the other women he has come across. I was getting physically tired by then and also tired of the turn that the conversation seemed to have taken and couldn't wait for the dinner to end.

THE DAYS ARE FLYING

Adam is in Nay Pyi Taw today, so I am on my own again, but I don't mind. A girl was terminated for a social media posting and the termination was done without consulting legal. I have to ask Than Tun to translate the posting and I remind him of the sensitivity and confidentiality of the situation. He assures me that he is well-acquainted with the rules with regard to human resource matters.

As I prepare to leave the office, I realise I am in no mood to go out again and I send the gang a text cancelling my outing with them and saying we should try to catch up another time. The truth is, I am very tired. I wake up every night now again and I have gone back to hearing that blasted monk band. Adam texts that he will be back from Nay Pyi Taw midmorning and thanks me for holding down the fort. I respond and wish him safe travels on his return.

I finally leave the office at 7 p.m. The days feel like they are flying by. It is pouring, but my faithful taxi driver is standing outside the building waiting for me. The taxi drivers are having a discussion among themselves as my driver sends another taxi driver to get an umbrella. But then he asks me if I have an umbrella, and, when I say yes, he tells his taxi driver colleague not to bother and points me to the car. I know that Yangon is far from being a palace, but these taxi drivers make me feel like royalty and I am so grateful for the way they look after me. Than Tun thinks that the special treatment I receive from the taxi drivers is because they charge me tourist prices, but I don't mind. They will definitely be one of the fixtures in my stay in Yangon that I will miss when my stint here is over.

I keep telling everyone that the best part of Yangon is the people. I am fortunate I got to be here before they are too tainted by the Western world. When I reach the hotel, I immediately go and order my dinner before going to my room. I am so tired that I know if I go up I will not come back down, and I will not get to eat dinner. While I am going through the menu, I get a message from Sean and I remember that I never got around to responding to his initial message. Earlier in the day he asked if I had given any thought to the future. I tell him that I have chosen to return to Barbados and I will confirm it to the team here tomorrow. I try not to think too much about it.

As I get back to my hotel, I realise I am getting a Skype call from Nicole so I dig my iPad out of my bag. Nicole is too cute. She tells me not to replace her and Keisha with random people. I laugh because I know she is referring to the profile picture I have put up on Blackberry messenger of Jennifer, Kristin, Ava and me. She tells me about her time in New York — she is just back from a seminar — and I tell her how grateful I am for the opportunities that my company has given me. She asks what everyone's job is and I tell her. I explain to her that age doesn't matter with the company; they encourage you to reach your full potential.

Before we end our conversation, she urges me to hurry up and return to Barbados as she doesn't understand what is happening with the Malaysia Airlines flights. A Malaysian Airlines flight was shot down over the Ukraine-Russian border recently. This is the second incident involving Malaysia Airlines over the space of a few months. The first being the mysterious disappearance of a flight that was headed to

China. I took Malaysia Airlines from London to Malaysia and then from KL to Yangon. My flights are already booked and I have to do the reverse on Malaysia Airlines on the way back, but I am not worried.

ROOFTOP BAR AND MOJO

Friday, July 18, 2014

I meet up with Finn at breakfast. He is slightly concerned that he has just dropped his fork on his pants and it is his last set of clean clothes. Johnathan has messaged him saying that some of the people who were attending the conference were on the Malaysia Airlines plane that was shot down. Finn tells me that only yesterday morning he confirmed his flights back to Ireland via Malaysia on Malaysia Airlines. I tell him I am using them to fly to KL and London when I leave Yangon as well.

At the office, U Nu tells me that Than Tun is ill and won't make it in today. I exclaim *"Nga bar lote ya ma lell?"* (What am I going to do?) and they all laugh. I do rely heavily on Than Tun. Who will translate for me? The bell rings again today and we all cheer especially loudly because it is by no means a small feat as it has been raining now for days on end. I want the construction team to meet their targets and I want us to fulfil our obligations to the customer.

I have to take a break to go to the bathroom. Khin Papa, who also works in site acquisition and is friends with Htet Htet and Su, is there and she uses the honorific "Ma" before my name which means "little sister" in Burmese and asks me how I spend my weekends. I tell her they are usually very quiet and I tell her where I have been since I got here. She asks me if I like bars and I tell her, "Sometimes". She tells me I should contact her and we should go together. It is very sweet of her. She writes her number on a Post-it Note and tells me to call her anytime if I need anything. I am considering taking the train around Yangon on the upcoming weekend and think I may give her a call to see if she would like to join me. Than Tun had suggested earlier in the week that Sunday may be a better day to take the train.

Adam is back from Nay Pyi Taw and I remind him that he needs to review the resolutions I sent him so we can open new bank accounts for the railway tender bid as the CFO wants to do this when he returns from his visa run in Bangkok. After lunch, when things have settled down a bit, I tell Adam that I will not be staying in Yangon past the three-month secondment. I tell him that my job in the Eastern Caribbean is more in line with my career goals and he nods his head in understanding.

It is Friday evening and the gang cannot wait to kick back. We decide to go to the Vista Bar. It is supposed to be this really cool rooftop bar in Yangon, but I have learnt not to get my hopes up. Close to evening time Jane and the CEO invite us to join them at the Yangon Sailing Club, but we take a rain check as we have been there before and we have already made plans for Vista. Adam, Finn and I ride together and Elliot, Su, Htet Htet and Vlado will join us there. We send our bags back to the hotel with our driver Chok. I really can't imagine what a rooftop bar in Yangon will be like since the majority of the buildings are old and crumbling and the ones that are not are being newly constructed or renovated. I am also imagining that it will be very hot on the rooftop since Yangon is hot and humid. But the bar exceeds my expectations. It is quite cool on the rooftop and the sky is blazing with a sea of glorious hues of reds, oranges and pinks. I don't have enough words to describe this magic. The sun finally dips below the horizon and is replaced with twinkling building lights. We have a stunning view of the Shwedagon Pagoda. There is loud house music playing. The food is only okay, but this is Yangon and I am thankful because it could be hit or miss. Kwame joins us about an hour after we arrive. He is dancing and they all think his exaggerated dance moves are hilarious and rightfully so. Others not in our group have stopped to watch him dance. He notices them watching him and shows off his moves even more by bending his knees so he is almost touching the floor on a few occasions. When Kwame is done with being king of the dance floor, he resumes his seat and joins in the conversation. He gives his honest opinion of Myanmar and says if he had money he wouldn't be here. Everyone tends to sugarcoat it and say how wonderful it is. The people are lovely, but it has years of catching up to do. He leaves us at around 9 p.m. because he has to make a Skype call. We bid him goodbye and have some more fun.

When we have had our fill of Vista, we take a taxi to Mojo. There are six of us by now and, instead of taking two cabs, Elliot insists on us taking one. Finn rushes into the front seat and Adam and Elliot ride in the boot. It is like a scene from Flintstones. Now, the last time we were at Mojo we had worked out that we have to have a few drinks before we actually get there, so we are all well tipsy by the time we arrive.

Mojo is an industrial chic cocktail bar and lounge. If you go late it is more of a nightclub vibe so be prepared to dance. Sometimes there is a live band, other times it is just the DJ spinning the latest tracks. Having a few drinks before puts you in the mood and eliminates the warming up period for your drunken interactions. If you arrive entirely sober, you may realise that you don't want to be there at all. We head upstairs and the place is packed. Marcus is there as well. I begin to feel tired close to 2 a.m., so I say goodbye to everyone and catch a taxi back to the hotel. When I arrive, I ask the front desk attendants for my bag, but they say no bags are there. I again inquire if they are sure no one left bags. There should have been three bags. They say no. I am too tired to even get upset or try to press them any further. I try to think about what is in my bag apart from my laptop and my glasses and I decide that there isn't anything that I immediately need from the bag. I figured maybe the driver misunderstood us and took the bags home with him. I ask them for a new room key since my room key is in the bag and I go to my room and crash.

APARTMENT HUNTING

Saturday, July 19, 2014

When I wake up the battery on my Myanmar phone is running low and my Barbados phone is completely dead. I decide to put them to charge and wait until a decent hour to text Adam and Finn about the bags. I am feeling the effects of too much drinking and too many cigarettes.

Finn texts me at about 8:35 a.m. to tell me that my bag is still in the luggage room under Room 418. It seems like the driver left them under Adam's name. He then texts again asking for a favour — he wants a second opinion on some apartments he will be viewing as he is staying for six months and it is not ideal to be living in a hotel for that long. Even though I am dog tired and hungover, I tell him sure and we plan to meet at 9 a.m. for breakfast as the agent is supposed to arrive at 9:30.

I go down for 9 a.m. and take down my laundry, fetch my bag and head to the breakfast area. I see Evan there so I end up sitting with him. He asks how I am and I tell him that I am slightly hungover. He asks where we went and I tell him Vista and Mojo and he says he went to Café Libre instead. I finish breakfast and wait for Finn in the lobby and he arrives soon after. The agent joins us not long after that and we leave the hotel to go see apartments. This is my first time going to see apartments in Yangon. The first place we visit has betel nut stains on the staircase. When the agent finally shows us the actual apartment, it is a definite no. We see two more and I am not sure if the agent understood what Finn is looking for.

When we get back to our hotel, we make plans to meet up with Jane at Union Bar later. It is Saturday night, and when we arrive at Union Bar there is Latin dancing. After our meal and when we've had enough of watching the dancers, Finn and I say goodbye to Jane and we go back to Mojo. We can't seem to get enough of Mojo.

Sunday, July 20, 2014

It is Sunday morning and, after a weekend of barhopping and drinking, I am amazed that I can get up and get myself together to meet Finn at 11 a.m. for another round of apartment viewing. Finn is late today after giving out to the agent yesterday for showing up late for their appointment. The apartments have features unique to Asian countries like a wet kitchen and a dry kitchen (not equipped with a sink). There are also windowless, cupboard-sized rooms for domestic helpers' living quarters, should you choose to have one. However, some of the layouts are quite awkward and others are just poorly constructed to begin with despite the high price tags. Landlords in Yangon know that there is a demand for expat housing so they can set any price they like. The furnishings are not modern and of varying quality. As the day goes on, I think Finn comes to the realisation that he will have to adjust his expectations and not measure the apartments by Western standards too much. As I watch Finn's obvious frustration, I am secretly glad that I don't have to go through the stress of finding an apartment for myself. In Myanmar, if you are renting a place for six months to a year, all the rent has to be paid upfront in cash and in US dollars for the entire period, so there is always the risk that once the landlord has your money he won't bother to respond to your calls if anything stops working. After viewing, we have lunch and then return to the hotel to sleep. I wash my hair first, but I am wrecked from partying two nights in a row. How I managed it in my teens and early twenties is beyond me.

CHANGING ROOMS

Monday, July 21, 2014

I notice mould on my shoes in the closet of my hotel room. By Monday night when I have returned from the office, I discover it has travelled to my clothes. That would explain why my skin started itching me a few days ago. I had dismissed it as the humidity triggering my eczema and tried not to behave like an alarmist or prima donna.

I send everything to the laundry and request that I get a different room. However, the hotel says no more rooms are available and they will try and have me moved tomorrow. In the meantime, they advise me to pack up everything and bring them down to the luggage room in the morning.

Tuesday, July 22, 2014

I wake up earlier than usual and get dressed in a set of clothes that I had left folded in my suitcase since there was no more room in the closet. I am actually thankful at this moment as if they had fit in the closet then I don't know what I would be wearing today. I take my fold-up ballet flats that I like to call my "fast flats" out of my handbag where I usually keep them and I put them on. I didn't have much else to pack except some toiletries, my electronics and a few pieces of casual clothing that I kept in another set of drawers. I take my clothes off the hangers in the closet, place them in a few laundry bags and take them down to reception. I also give them the shoes that the mould has travelled to as they need to be cleaned as well.

Finn and I go to the Yangon Bakehouse at lunchtime and see Adam there with Su. I am surprised that he did not bother to invite us, but I suppose we are all entitled to not inviting each other sometimes. Our little community sometimes reminds me of the sitcom *Friends* with our friendship dynamics, our sometimes-comedic adventures, essentially what has become of our lives during this time. I get a text from Adam later asking if I got the room changed and I respond with "Yes I did, thanks."

Wednesday, July 23, 2014

At lunch time, Adam, Su and I take a walk with Elliot who wants to join the gym. I have zero interest in the gym, but I take the walk for a change of scenery. Also, there is an eatery next to the gym, so we decide before setting off that we are going to try there for lunch once Elliot finishes his signing up. When we get there, however, the eatery is closed for renovations so we end up going back to Golden Pearl.

Later in the day Khin Marla sends the email with information regarding my visa run. It seems like it will be a very time-consuming process. I am only half looking forward to going to Bangkok because of all this visa stuff that has to be taken care of first. The CFO sends me passport scans for all the authorised signatories of the company and I am amused to see that he actually had hair on his head in his picture.

THE DAY YOU WERE BORN

Thursday, July 24, 2014

We have a team lunch and they think I do not like the food because I am not eating loads and Mima reveals that she is not convinced that I like Myanmar. I assure her that I do and the best part of Yangon for me is the team. She asks when I am leaving Yangon and I tell her that I am leaving at the end of August. She asks why so soon and, when I tell her because I have to go back to my job, she says that they will miss me.

It is the first time I feel guilty about leaving. Adam is leaving today to return to Melbourne. It was only today that I learnt there are plans to reduce the current number of expats so Noah may just have been a casualty of war. I am reminded again that in Yangon everyone seems to be just passing through.

At lunch the girls teach me that the people of Myanmar place great value in their cultural traditions on the day that you were born. The conversation starts because the restaurant's menu is more like a book and, besides the food options, it has an astrology chart on it with a detailed reading about the day you were born. The day that one was born is most important in daily life in Myanmar. Every individual soul is named after the day that he or she is born. In Myanmar's history there is no family name since Burmese people do not carry family names. As such, your other family members may be born different days of the week and all will have different names. Myanmar people strongly believe in astrology and the day you are born plays a major factor in telling your fate, matchmaking, business dealing, household building and even buying a car or applying for a job.

Burmese consult with astrologers or Buddhist monks who then refer to their birthday to tell them the dos and don'ts. Myanmar chronology defines eight days in a week, with Wednesday being divided into morning and evening. Wednesday evening is called "Yarhu". However, Yarhu is not considered a significant day of the week and it is not printed in the calendars. Mima explained that the eight days are represented by eight cardinal points in every pagoda and you worship at the point which represents your birthday. Normally at each corner there is a Buddha statute on a small shrine where you can worship, pour water and light candles.

I was born on a Monday so the tiger is my symbol. An interpretation of my sign on the menu says: "You are very intelligent and intuitive. You have a keen eye for detail. You are strong and patient, but only to a point. You detest being taken advantage of and you don't like people wasting your time. You are goal-oriented and like to succeed. You are respectful of laws and take responsibility for your actions." I have to admit — this sounds exactly like me.

IT'S A SMALL WORLD

Friday, July 25, 2014

Adam isn't here today. He is back in Melbourne. It isn't as crazy as I thought it would be, even though everyone is coming to me for everything. I see a message from my cousin asking if I met his friend Yvonne in a nail spa in Yangon. I tell him yes, but explain that I misplaced the card she had given me with her contact details. He gives me her email address and tells me that she is leaving Yangon on Sunday and wants to invite me to a party. What a small world it is!

It is Friday, but I am not sure what everyone else is doing later. I am not too keen on going out to drink anyway. I make a 6:30 p.m. appointment to get a French gel manicure done. These simple things keep me happy in Yangon. When my nails are finished, I text Finn to find out what he is doing even though I do not really want to go out. I do not hear from him and I am content to head back to the hotel.

Even though I have to go into the office tomorrow I am happy it is Friday as Saturdays in the office are a bit more relaxed. When I arrive back at the hotel, reception gives me my new room key and says that my suitcases, laundry and shoes have already been delivered to my new room. My new room is exactly two doors away from my old room and looks exactly the same. When I have had my shower and changed, I go down to have dinner. I see Evan in the lobby after dinner and I chat with him about his week. I tell him I have confirmed to Adam that I am going home after the three months are up. He comments that the Caribbean is better than Yangon and then he starts chatting about the time he was in the Galapagos Islands and how he wished he had taken that opportunity to go to the Caribbean islands as well. While we are chatting, one of the hotel staff members hands him a letter over the reception desk and he pauses to read it. I jokingly ask him if it is a letter from Kitty, his Burmese girlfriend, and to my surprise he confirms that it is. He then tells me about the incident earlier in the week when she came to his hotel room pounding loudly on the door because she felt that he was sleeping with her friend. I don't ask him if she was right. I really don't care enough to ask, but I wouldn't put it past him. The letter basically says that she understands he wants nothing to do with her and she is letting him go. He heads outside to have a beer and I, having finished my dinner, head back up the stairs to enjoy a quiet evening in.

GAELIC FOOTBALL
IN MYANMAR

Saturday, July 26, 2014

Jane and Farrell have invited Finn and me to a Gaelic football match that is being played this afternoon around three. I wasn't going to go initially since it was raining and going to bed sounded more appealing, but then I thought, what the hell, don't start being boring now, Nadia. I had vaguely remembered from my Irish colleagues in the Caribbean that Gaelic football is a type of football played in Ireland.

Each team has fifteen players and there is one referee. It is played with a circular ball on a rectangular pitch with H-shaped goals at each end. Both hands and feet are used to pass the ball. It sounded to me like a hybrid of American football and soccer. There was no way that I was going to wear what I was currently wearing, so I went back to the hotel, traded my work attire for a pair of jeans, a cute baby-T and my nude flats and came back to meet Jane and the others. The Gaelic football pitch is near the Pun Hlaing Golf Estate and I haven't been out that way yet so I think that it would be good to see it. I remember when I was researching Myanmar that was one of the areas I wanted to live until I found out it was a significant distance from the location of the office.

Jane had got us a few bags of chips from Lotteria (a South Korean fast-food chain) for lunch and a few cokes and we eat in the car on the way to the golf course. When we are finished eating, we all take various sections of a bid we must read for work. I end up with the executive summary and some other sections. There is no such thing as a free lunch or a free ride. The drive is a long one in traffic and I am reminded that Myanmar is a huge place.

The match is Myanmar against Singapore. Three matches will be played today actually: a women's match, a men's match and a mixed-team match. When we get there, I am surprised to see that Marcus is warming up in a yellow and green uniform and he is playing for the Myanmar team. He is easy to spot as he is the only black person on the team. I am always happy to see Marcus. He has such great energy. Finn and I decide to go over to where the team is warming up to say hello to Marcus and to wish him good luck. As we get closer, I realise that Matt is also playing for the Myanmar team. I immediately adjust my walk to strolling over as sexily as I can muster while trying not to slip in the mud and fall flat on my face. I say hi to Matt nonchalantly and he comes over and kisses me on both cheeks. I introduce Matt to Finn and then we engage in some minor chitchat which includes them trying to recruit Finn and me. The men practice on Tuesday evenings, they explain, and there is a women's team as well. Without committing to anything, we bid Matt and Marcus goodbye so they can continue with their warm-up as the game will soon start and we head over to the line where the spectators are.

It is a big crowd despite the weather. I had no idea that so many people were interested in Gaelic football. The referee sounds the whistle and the players take their positions. Then the referee throws the ball up between four midfielders (two from either side) and the game starts. The pitch is a sea of yellow and green (the Myanmar team) and red and white (the Singapore team). They are all jostling for the ball and slipping and sliding all over the place. Occasionally, a few players are able to break out and get what seems like an actual game going with proper passing and advancing towards the H-shaped bars, but then it descends into chaos again. This continues for the first few minutes and then the game is briefly interrupted by a lashing of rain and we all scamper to take cover under the pavilion. We meet up again with Farrell who has actually also been sheltering at the pavilion the entire time. When the rain finally stops, we return to the sideline and the players return to an even muddier pitch and the game resumes. Marcus breaks free and passes to Matt who passes to another player and the Myanmar team almost scores. The ladies are all cheering for Marcus (the Gals Dem Sugar). Occasionally the Myanmar team comes close to scoring and there is clapping and cheering and the shouting of various players' names, but mostly it is the Singapore team which has possession and ultimately wins the game. During the match I smoke and drink and generally enjoy myself. I am glad I didn't go back to the hotel to sleep after all. This experience was definitely worth the sacrifice. As we are leaving, I look down and notice, not for the first time, that my attempts to keep my feet clean were futile. There are mud smudges in the area by my ankles and on my nude flats. Before jumping into the vehicle, I wash off my feet with the bottled water that we had left in the vehicle with the driver. I feel slightly guilty for doing this when people have no drinking water. On the way back I realise that the golf course is close to FMI City where Mark and Lucia live.

ALL ABOUT THE POLITICS

Sunday, July 27, 2014

I speak to my aunt Jean in New York and she is well. I enjoy talking to her because she always has some funny story about her life in New York. She wants to come and visit me in Myanmar and I am excited about the possibility of having a visitor. God bless her. She is the most adventurous one in my family.

I enjoy my relaxing Sunday and go downstairs to have dinner. I end up eating with Lily who is Danish, slightly plump with blonde hair, and Damon who is Irish and plump with black hair. They both work in finance. Dinner with them is generally pleasant and not boring at all even if they are only finance people.

Monday, July 28, 2014

Purely by coincidence, Lily and I end up riding together to work. We were both leaving the hotel at the same time and decided to share a taxi. We get to chatting some more and I discover that even though she is

Danish, she left Denmark with her mother and brother when she was a child and moved to Australia. She says it was lovely to have dinner with Damon and me last night instead of on her own. We discuss some of the challenges of being single, expat and female. The reality of the dating scene here is that Western men are seen as good catches by many Asian women, while Western females are plagued with stereotypes such as being too independent and ripe for cultural friction (read not subservient enough) when it comes to Asian men. The available Western men have their pick of younger Asian women, so why would they want to date a Western woman? The other issue is that many men prefer the naturally slim figure of Asian women versus other body types and there are myriad issues related to race and gender, one is that of men being paid more for the same expat posting as a female. When we reach the office, we bid each other goodbye as she heads to the Finance Department and I head to the Legal Department.

When I arrive, my team is discussing politics. They are having a heated debate and it is strange for me to hear them like this as they are generally quiet. Of course, I do not understand everything they are saying. Than Tun explains to me that they are discussing the fact that the country is in the third phase of development. The first phase of development started in 2008. He says that things have improved significantly, but there is still a long way to go. I understand what he is saying, but these things take time. I ask him if he has ever considered being involved in politics. He tells me he has and explains that he has even taken a few classes and has been involved with an activist group. I tell him that he would make a good politician. He tells me that Khing Sa also wants to be a politician and I say that I think that Khing Sa would make a good politician, as well as Win Tin. He says Win Tin doesn't want to be a good politician, just a good businessman. I think they are well-placed to effect the change that their country needs.

A COLD, A VISA
AND BAD NEWS

Wednesday, July 30, 2014

Things have been pretty hectic in the office today, so I just have enough time to grab lunch from the Yangon Bakehouse. I order a small Texas bean chilli soup and half a sandwich on a baguette which cost me K6,000. I have a cold and Than Tun notices and gives me 500mg Vitamin C. I have never experienced such kindness even in my own country. I love the team to bits. I have morphed into living a very unhealthy lifestyle – drinking, smoking, not running and not taking care of myself like I used to – and this could be the reason I find myself with a cold.

Today I have to go to the Thai Embassy in Yangon to get a visa to enter Thailand so that I can go to the Myanmar Embassy in Thailand and get a visa to re-enter Myanmar. My business visa will expire soon as it has only been issued for seventy days and my secondment period is for ninety days. There is no visa extension mechanism so I will need to get a new visa. When I get to the Thai Embassy, an embassy officer tells me all of the numbers for the day have already been issued and I should come back tomorrow. I tell her that I cannot come back tomorrow and that I need to get the visa today. She takes my passport and tells me to return at 3 p.m. I ask her about paying and she says that I should pay when I return. However, I am hesitant to leave my visa with a stranger without anything to show that I handed it over to her. I ask if I get a receipt and she assures me that "we are safe" and that I shouldn't worry. I again experience that feeling I got when I had to hand over my passport in Malaysia. It is not a good feeling, but I am hopeful I will get back my passport and my visa at 3 p.m.

I go back to the office. Today is the deadline for submitting a request for quotation (RFQ) document for another operator. The deadline is 4 p.m. and I am asked to join the team in the boardroom. I make my contribution and I am happy to be involved. We are under lots of pressure. I am not sure how we have found ourselves working under such pressure as we thought we had everything under control. As it turns out, the document needed a lot more work than we had anticipated. Thank God that the additional work to be done did not fall under the Legal Department's purview. The CFO is getting antsy because he has to go and collect his kids. At 2:30 p.m. I excuse myself from the group, content that we have secured a day's extension to submit the RFQ. When I reach the Thai Embassy it is 2:55 p.m. and they allow me to go right in. However, instead of being able to collect my visa, I am told to pay US$40 and return tomorrow at 1:30 p.m. to collect. I will have to sleep tonight without my passport.

The bell rings today. We are getting there slowly but surely. The bell ringing used to be more frequent when I first got here.

Since Finn had a bad experience with the pasta at the hotel, I am reluctant to have dinner there this evening and, instead, I call Marcus and tell him to come eat with me at The Lab. They serve tapas there. While I am getting ready to go, I look at my phone and realise that I have received a text that an acquaintance whom I met through work in Barbados died of a heart attack. We were not close, but we were always friendly to each other and had socialised outside of work on a few occasions. I feel a pang of sadness, but I resist the urge to cancel my plans to meet Marcus as I know he will lift my spirits. It is a bit strange, though, being away from home when something tragic happens and not having your usual support around.

I reach The Lab and Marcus is already there. He introduces me to the owner of the establishment and some other people he knows, telling them I am from Barbados. We sit at the bar as the place is packed and order some food and drinks. We talk about any and everything. I even try to gather intelligence from him on Matt, but all he can tell me is Matt already has a girlfriend.

Thursday, July 31, 2014

I finally secure my visa for Bangkok and we get the RFQ submitted. Praises be to Jah. Adam sends me a WhatsApp message to say his doctors found two cancers — in addition to the skin cancer, they discover cancer cells in his nose. He is all bandaged up after the surgery, so he hasn't had a chance to see what he looks like yet. I hope he is okay and there are no complications. I think he should rest and not worry about what is going on over here and I tell him as much.

CELEBRATIONS

Friday, August 1, 2014

I am thankful that it is the end of the week, even though I have to be in tomorrow. One thing I can safely say is that I will not miss working on Saturdays when I return home. There was a mobile launch earlier today and SIM cards were issued to our company. The launch marks the first time that affordable telecommunications services have been made accessible to Myanmar's people.

It is also the first time in the country's history that access to the internet via a mobile device has been widely available. Of the SIM cards provided for the company, however, only four have been allocated to the Legal Department and I have more than four lawyers on my team. It was suggested that they draw lots, but I decide that I would purchase the additional SIM cards for the rest of my team. It is a small team, after all, and I don't want some persons on the team to have and others to be without. Each SIM cost only K5,000 so I don't mind buying the additional ones out of my own pocket. It is a small gesture since they have been such a great team. When I deliver the SIM cards to them, they are all very excited and say thank you. I am happy to be involved in this little slice of history. I understand how much it means to my team and the people of Myanmar as a whole since telecommunications were formerly tightly controlled by the military junta with the government monopolising the sector and selling SIM cards for thousands of dollars. To give you an idea, under the junta rule a SIM card, if it could be sourced, could cost in the range of US$1,000. It was an extravagance only the rich and well-connected could afford. When the nominal civilian government took over, the SIM prices were still a whopping US$250 and still expensive for the average Burmese.

I end up going to Vista Rooftop Bar after work, but I leave early as I am battling a cold. I see a message from Marcus later that he is headed to a reggae party at 50th Street, but I turn back over and go back to sleep.

Saturday, August 2, 2014

It is Saturday and I get to lie in a bit longer this morning. This evening is a celebratory dinner at Western Park Royal Restaurant for the role our company played in the successful mobile launch. I decide on an elegantly-styled short, printed three-quarter-sleeve shirt dress that falls nicely just above the knees. I choose this dress since the length is flattering with the right amount of sexy and sophistication and the three-quarter sleeves will keep me warm and cosy as it is a hotel and the air conditioning is likely to be blasting. Very few places seem to get the temperature balance right. I choose my nude peep toe heels for the occasion. The Western Park Royal Restaurant is six minutes away from our hotel, so I take a taxi with Finn. Johnathan will follow us later as he takes his time getting dressed.

When we arrive at the restaurant, I am happy that all of my team is there. A few of them even end up at the same table with me — Win Tin and his wife, Ne Win, Nu Nu and Htun Htun. The meal consists of various Chinese dishes. It is an enjoyable night and I get further insight into Myanmar culture. After dinner, the girls even pull me up on stage for the Myanmar traditional dance which I know nothing about. However, they tell me not to worry because they will teach me. Luckily, the moves aren't too complicated and I follow closely and mimic what they are doing, which is mostly hand gestures and touching the feet on the ground lightly.

Sunday, August 3, 2014

I end up going to brunch with Finn and Johnathan at the Inya Lake Hotel. There is unlimited sparkling wine so that is the attraction. We arrive just before 11 a.m. and finally leave at 4 p.m. We end up buying our own bottle of sparkling wine after the time for the unlimited sparkling wine ends. I have an enjoyable time with them. They are great together and keep me in fits of laughter. I love them to death. I finally have, not one, but two gay friends. Every woman's dream.

Monday, August 4, 2014

It is Kadooment Day in Barbados and I am feeling nostalgic and yearning a little for home. I want to join in the festivities with Keisha and the band. I am, however, looking forward to finally going to Bangkok. Adam had to push out his return date and therefore he won't be able to manage the department while I am away. He felt that he should stay in Melbourne and take more time to heal. I miss his presence in the office, but I am happy he is choosing to take care of himself. I send an email to Murray informing him that since Adam has pushed out his return date to Thursday both of us will be physically absent on Wednesday but that he should contact me on my Barbados mobile if he needs me. He knows about the visa run; we all have to do it.

VISA RUN TO BANGKOK

Tuesday, August 5, 2014

Today is the long-awaited day! Su and I have become close friends and she is going with me to Bangkok. She has never been before, so, when I told her about my visa run, I suggested that she come along with me. I am a bit anxious as the main reason I am going to Bangkok is to get my visa and Khin Marla seems to think that it will take three days. However, I am determined that this will not take three days. I plan to get this over and done with in a day so that I can enjoy the rest of my time in Bangkok.

Su and I decide to meet up at the airport, but she is late in reaching the airport as she is trying to wrap up a few things before she leaves the office. I try to explain to her that the company will be fine. They will all live for a few days while she is away. She is a worrywart. I meet Chris from Chicago while I am in the line waiting to check in. He notices my blue passport and asks where I am from since the usual colour of the passports on this side of the world is red. He is retired and looking to set up an assembly plant in Myanmar. As we finish our conversation, I see Su hustling toward me. She has finally arrived. We complete our check-in and head toward the security area. When we pass through that stage, she rings her mother and the kids one last time and we wait until it is time to board our flight.

Su and I arrive after an uneventful flight and I discover that Bangkok is a huge contrast to Myanmar. Bangkok is loud, bustling, smoky and even more humid than Yangon. We secure a taxi outside of the airport and we are on our way. Along the way there are rows of modern skyscrapers and colourful Buddhist temples next to them. We pass rows of condo buildings with a few palm trees next to them. As we continue on our drive, the last remaining light fades, it starts to rain and the roads are congested with traffic. After about two hours of slowly crawling through the traffic, we finally arrive at the Mode Sathorn Hotel and the driver tries to scam us by asking us to pay more than we should have to. We are not having it. We have already paid the tolls and will only pay the amount on the meter. We finally despatch the unpleasant taxi driver and make our way to the front desk for check-in. Because I prepaid for the hotel stay, check-in is done quickly and I am able to get to bed early since I have to be at the embassy very early in the morning.

Wednesday, August 6, 2014

I am the first one in line at the embassy. As planned, I rose early and headed down to the lobby while Su is still fast asleep in the second bedroom of our suite. The guy at the front desk had looked at me a bit strangely when I told him that I wanted a taxi to the Myanmar Embassy. His answer was, "Now?" and I responded in the affirmative. I suppose he was a little confused since it was only 7:30 a.m. and the embassy didn't open until 9 a.m., but I was determined to be the first one in line when the doors open. I have all of my documents ready and I am later joined by backpackers and various other persons. Before the doors open at 8:30 a.m. about forty other people are lined up behind me. The office staff start taking applications at 9:00 a.m. and once I get that part out of the way I go back to the hotel to meet Su.

As I enter our hotel room, I realise that Su is fully dressed and excited to get out the hotel and see Bangkok. This is why she is here, after all. After a quick change, we go downstairs to the lobby and the hotel staff help us navigate the BTS Skytrain map and we decide to go to the Siam Paragon shopping mall. We have a great time shopping and then make a stop in the mall's food court for a little lunch. I have genuine Thai green curry which is so hot that it brings tears to my eyes. At around 2:30 p.m. we make our way back to the hotel to put down our things so that I can get back to the embassy around 3 p.m. for my 3:30 p.m. visa collection. When I get there, a handful of people are already waiting outside. There are a lot of migrant workers waiting on the opposite side of the street as well. When they see the embassy worker approaching the building, they all flock over and enter once the doors are opened. Since I am coughing so much — the symptoms of this stubborn cold just wouldn't give me a break — one of the guys in line tells me to sit on the chair and he will hold my space in line. This is very kind of him and I am again amazed by the kindness of total strangers. I get back my passport with my visa in what seems like record time and head back to the hotel.

I would have been happy to just stay in the hotel and rest because of this cold, but Su wants to go out. The first bar that she chooses is closed so we end up walking a long way and taking a tuk tuk (a motorised rickshaw with three wheels) part of the way to reach the Sky Bar at Lebua which is one of the highest rooftop bars in the world at 820 feet in the air and is shaped like a dome. At the dome bar I am thrilled to experience the flickering city lights and backlight bar that changes colour throughout the night, the most delicious spicy tuna rolls, California rolls and rainbow rolls and several Sky Bar "Hangovertini" cocktails. I thoroughly enjoy Lebua. Apparently, it is where the movie *Hangover 2* was filmed, hence the name of the cocktail. It was well worth the walk and uncomfortable tuk tuk ride. I make a mental note to watch Hangover 2 again.

Thursday, August 7, 2014

I am able to lie in later since the visa was all taken care of yesterday. I would again be grateful to just stay at the hotel, but Su wants to explore. We decide on the MBK Shopping Centre and Siam Paragon again. MBK is a bit of a disappointment. Due to its reputation for lower prices it was more packed with locals and tourists, more frenetic than Siam Paragon and the disordered atmosphere meant we couldn't really find any shops that we wanted to spend time in. It is definitely not a mall for strolling around in and looking, so we quickly give up and spend the rest of the afternoon at a more civilised, leisurely and relaxing pace at Siam Paragon. Later, we have dinner at the hotel since I started feeling poorly and we go to bed by 10 p.m. or so as we are being picked up at 6:30 a.m. for a tour to the Damnoen Saduak Floating Market. According to the brochure, the market is 100 km southwest of Bangkok.

THE FLOATING MARKET

Friday, August 8, 2014

The colours, chaos, atmosphere and scenes make the Floating Market the single best experience I have had in all of Asia. As the boat speeds down the waterway, the only noise is that of the engine and the light chatter of the other passengers as we zoom past small wooden houses on stilts on the river banks. One of the tourists in the boat asks the driver if he can go slower. The boat driver slows down and we catch a glimpse of a snake in the water.

The sight of the snake startles me and I hold on to Su and she laughs. We get a glimpse of some of the people who live on the river and are going about their daily business. Most are oblivious to us, but a few children wave. I breathe and soak it all in. He speeds up again and we soon see the entrance for the market in the distance. The journey in the colourful long-tail boat from the pier to the market takes about twenty minutes. There is a line of similar long-tail boats entering the market. Once we are inside the canals, we are transferred to smaller boats which are rowed predominantly by women. It is 9 a.m. now and the sun is already beating down. The rower takes us to the smaller canals first and eventually into the main canal. The wares are displayed on the boats and on both sides of the canal.

I am not at all prepared for what I see, given the relative quiet journey in the long-tail boat. The market is colourful and noisy and crowded with boats of tourists and sellers rowing their boats and selling everything from fruits and vegetables, to fried rice, mini coconut pancakes and boat noodles in a rich broth. The boats bump into each other and there is a massive traffic jam on the water. A vendor on land takes a large stick and frees the boats. This happens more than a few times since the waterway is very crowded. When the rower thinks we have had enough, she pulls the boat close to the canal banks and, as we step off the boat, there is a young Thai man — probably in his twenties — with a huge yellow snake wrapped around his neck. He asks if we want to hold it. No, thank you. We find ourselves among busy stalls selling small toy elephants, food, tiger balms and a variety of clothes and souvenirs. Since we both missed breakfast because we had to leave the hotel so early for the tour, we are beyond famished and, after Su and I walk around the market for a bit, we settle on a food stall that looks relatively popular and sit down on the benches close to it. A waiter brings us a plastic menu that is written in Thai, Chinese and English and thankfully has pictures. We order pad Thai (stir-fried noodles), satay, khao pad (fried rice) and some kluay tod (fried banana) and some coconut water to wash it all down.

I love Lin, our tour guide. She looks to be in her early thirties, but I can't be sure because Asian women have a way of naturally defying their age. She has the kindest hazel eyes and, when her smile reaches them, they turn into little slits below her eyebrows. Her hair seems to be piled up on her head in a loose one and is covered with a conical straw hat popular in Bangkok. She is very animated. Up until the point when we disembarked the boat to explore, she had not stopped chatting since she boarded the vehicle. When we return to the boat, she makes me laugh when she remarks that the movie *The King and I* is based on Thailand but it is banned in Thailand. She swears that Su is from Thailand and keeps calling her the Beautiful Thai Lady. After we leave the Floating Market, the tour takes us to an elephant farm and then we travel to a woodcarving centre where we eat coconut ice cream from a coconut shell.

Once we get back to the hotel which is thirty-eight floors high, I check out the infinity rooftop pool for a 360-degree view of the city, but it is too hot up there so I go back to our room and take a nap and then grab something to eat downstairs at the hotel. Around 5:30 p.m. Eric, a friend of Su's, comes to meet us and takes us to visit a number of places. We go to Patpong Night Market which is a popular night bazaar in Bangkok where you can buy anything from a fake Rolex to knockoff designer bags and shoes to street food. After that, we make our way to a Mexican restaurant (we dare not try the street food) where a ladyboy named Fee is our server and then we head to a club with live music. By the time we make it to Soi Cowboy — a street with a large number of go-go bars — it is almost midnight. Bangkok is a bustling, modern city with a happening night life and is in stark contrast to Myanmar. I still feel a little run-down as the cold continues its vice grip on me, but I do not regret getting out on the town with Su and Eric. Everyone should experience Bangkok at least once in their lives for the sheer number of experiences it offers.

RETURN TO YANGON

Saturday, August 9, 2014

We make it back to Yangon in one piece in spite of my cold. We are delighted to be greeted at the airport by Su's mother, her two daughters and the girls' nanny. On the ride to drop me off at my hotel in Yangon Su's daughters and their nanny are my backseat companions. At first the girls are shy and barely glance at me, but after a few minutes they warm up to me. Su's mother thanks me for looking after Su and bringing her back safely, but somehow I think Su was probably the one who looked after me.

Monday, August 11, 2014

On Sunday I decided to stay in bed all day and rest in an effort to recover from this cold that has been dogging me for much too long. To help me pass the time, I watch the movies *White House Down* and *Jack Frost*.

Today I am feeling a little better, but even though I am not 100% yet I make my way to the office. I have been away for long enough after spending the last few days of the week before in Bangkok. I am pleased to see Adam who is back from Melbourne and seems to be doing well after his surgeries. He asks me to stay in Yangon for another month, but I really can't. I am worried my job won't be there when I get back to the Eastern Caribbean if I stay any longer.

Wednesday, August 13, 2014

Tuesday was pretty much a typical day in the office, except that the cold still persists. I kept to myself most of the day and worked quietly. I came home feeling drained and miserable and was content to slip into my bed early.

Today I woke up and thanked God that I have been surrounded by such love for my time in Myanmar. Mima is a star. Yesterday she was so concerned about me that she brought me some Loratyn-10 and Bronchest to help me fight off the cold. The directions were not in English so she wrote out the dosage I should take in my notebook. I slept well last night thanks to the medicine. This morning she sent me a song that I liked. She says she wants me to be happy in Myanmar as I seem lonely. I think this is very sweet of her. Of course, I can sometimes be lonely even in Barbados, but at least Barbados is home and I am a bit more comfortable there. She calls me her sister and she says that she loves me. Such an outpouring of love makes me feel very emotional and I want to cry, but of course I do not cry in the office. Finn sent me a text this morning telling me that I am welcome to their pad to visit or stay once I am better. It is so kind of him as well. I think I may go next weekend as I have decided to go to Bagan this coming weekend.

A WEEKEND IN BAGAN

Saturday, August 16, 2014

My taxi driver Tu Wai was there at the hotel's main lobby to pick me up at 4:55 a.m. to take me to the airport for my 5:20 a.m. check-in. The side of the airport that handles domestic flights is very interesting. They place a sticker on you with the logo or name of the airline which you will be travelling on and then they hold up a sign with the name of the airline when it is time for you to board your flight and you assemble where the person holding the sign is standing. Naturally, there is no working Wi-Fi at the airport, so I entertain myself with people-watching.

Lots of tourists are heading to Bagan. An interracial couple sits near to me — the guy is black and the girl is white. The guy acknowledges me, no doubt because of my skin colour. While I sit, I observe dozens of families, old folks and young couples passing by. The different accents and languages are a bit heady. I have no idea what to expect on this flight since I have never even heard of this airline until now. We are finally allowed to board a bus to take us to our Air Bagan aircraft and an hour later we are touching down at the Nyang-U Airport. It is a small domestic airport and the pilot makes a three-point turn on the runway before taxiing to a stop near the small terminal building. We then board a bus which takes us from the aircraft to the terminal. Since I have no checked luggage, I whiz through immigration and customs. Bagan is considered an archaeological zone, so at the airport you have to pay US$15 before leaving the airport, similar to paying an entrance fee at a tourist attraction. I pay, collect my ticket and I go outside. A taxi guy asks me if I need a taxi and I tell him yes. His name is Tun Tun and he takes me to the Hotel @ Tharabar Gate which is located in Old Bagan, the ancient capital of the Burmese Empire.

Bagan looks like an enchanted land from a storybook. Unlike the rest of Myanmar, Bagan has no rainy season so the earth is brown and dry. It is quiet and ancient pagodas with stunning ancient architecture dot the landscape one after the other. They go on for as far as the eye can see. I spot a few horse cart drivers close to the hotel. We arrive at the hotel and Tun Tun charges me K6,000 for the ride. At the hotel, Than Tun's tour guide friend, Zaw Aung, is waiting with a sign with my name on it. I wave excitedly to him. When I get out of the taxi, he helps me to the hotel. I immediately notice that the hotel is beautiful, with lush green grounds and an inviting pool like an oasis after the dusty ride. The staff are very attentive and allow me to take an early check-in and a late check-out. Their hospitality and general warmness impress me. The hotel has the layout of a beach hotel with single-storey buildings of a bungalow style spread throughout expansive grounds with a large pool and sunbeds in the centre. Yet, beyond the hotel, instead of a beach, there are splendid sights of pagodas and temples. A girl takes my bag to my bungalow. The rooms have teak floors and Burmese furniture, high ceilings and hand-painted wall paintings.

When I return to the lobby, Than Tun's friend sets out the plan for the day and I am happy to let him take charge. It costs US$33 for the car to take me around and US$25 for the tour guide until sunset. Any description I give of the place will not do it justice. I can hardly believe that I get to witness it with my own eyes. Think Angkor Wat or Machu Picchu. Our first stop is the Ananda Temple, known as the Jewel of Bagan, which is five minutes away from the hotel. The view is breathtaking. After the Ananda Temple, we go to a series of pagodas and temples and I am in awe of Bagan.

My tour guide deposits me back to the hotel and I am truly happy to return after loads of photos and hours of exploring. He suggests we go to Mount Popa, an extinct volcano, on Sunday. I know this is an opportunity for him to make more money, but even though I had planned to just relax at the hotel on Sunday I happily oblige. I may never get back to Bagan, so soaking up this awesome experience trumps a little sleep and relaxation. Zaw Aung will come to collect me at 9 a.m.

MOUNT POPA AND
BYE BYE BAGAN

Sunday, August 17, 2014

It cost K45,000 for the car and US$27 for him for the day. I do not mind giving him the money because he explains to me that things are slow. On the way, we stop at a little village and I learn how to make palm oil from the toddy palm. The Burmese people use the palm oil to make various dishes. I also try some distilled whiskey from the toddy palm and pickled tea leaves which I actually enjoy.

The journey to Mount Popa is long, but I enjoy the drive through the countryside. People wave as the car goes by. I cannot help but wonder what their lives must be like in their little villages. As we drive along, I notice that all through the villages are signs which read "National League for Democracy". When I ask the tour guide, he tells me that is Aung San Suu Kyi's political party. She is currently the opposition leader, but the military generals changed the constitution so that she will never be president. We stop at Popa Market, which sells mostly fruits and vegetables. Popa is green in contrast to the rest of Bagan. Finally, we can see a golden temple glistening in the sun and looking quite majestic as it sits in its perched position on top a mountain. Zaw Aung tells me that is Mount Popa we are seeing.

Mount Popa is an extinct volcano. There are many Nat temples and relics there, so it is a popular pilgrimage site. Monkeys are all over and the guide warns me not to feed them. He also says I should hold my bag tightly as the monkeys have been known to run off with the bags of unsuspecting tourists. We are asked to remove our shoes at the entrance in order to climb the over seven hundred steps that snake to the peak of the temple. The guide tells me he will only climb a few of the steps as he has been to the top many times before and is feeling a bit tired today. The steps are easy enough to climb and there are many monkeys hanging around and hawkers selling souvenirs along the way to keep your company. At some parts during the ascent faithful worshippers are mopping and cleaning the steps. The guide tells me this is to increase good karma from Buddha. It's worth the climb as the views from the top are amazing.

I get back to the hotel at 1 p.m. and I am so happy I took the trip. Even though Bagan is definitely better than Mount Popa, at least I got to drive through the countryside on the way to Mount Popa and see a different side of Myanmar. The girls at the hotel reconfirm my flight. I was supposed to be travelling on Mann Yadanarpon Airlines for my return flight, but it turns out they codeshare with Air KBZ, a privately owned Burmese domestic airline, and my check-in time is now 4:00 p.m. instead of 4:40 p.m. so I will have to leave the hotel at 3:45 p.m. now instead of 4:15. The hotel arranges a taxi which is US$10 or K10,000 instead of the K6,000 which Tun Tun charged me. The taxi driver is pleasant enough. During the trip to the airport he asks where I am from, but he has no clue where Barbados is.

We repeat the same procedure here with the sticker as we did at the domestic section of Yangon International Airport. While I am in the departure lounge at the airport in Bagan a Korean man and his Yangon family strike up a conversation with me. He says that he is sure he saw me at Mount Popa earlier today. When I finish my chat with the Korean man, an Italian tourist sits next to me and also says she saw me climbing the steps at the temple. The flight back is uneventful. I am a bit tired and I was never so happy to see my taxi driver Tu Wai, a familiar face. He said, "I take you to your home in Yangon" when we reach the hotel. I smile and nod at his attempt to speak English to me. He is right — in many ways Yangon has become home to me.

BACK TO REALITY
AFTER BAGAN

Monday, August 18, 2014

Today I wear my yellow striped headband to work and the girls like it. Little do they know it is to hide my scruffy hair which hasn't been relaxed in three months!

I also have not washed my hair for the past week as I got back to Yangon late and I still have this stubborn cold. Luckily, I brought some dry shampoo with me from Barbados which seems to have done the trick. I will attempt to leave the office at a reasonable time and wash it this evening.

MY TRADITIONAL MYANMAR DRESS

Tuesday, August 19, 2014

I had to make a hard choice this morning. I had to choose between going to Inle Lake and staying in Yangon for my last weekend. I looked at pictures of Inle Lake and, while it is beautiful, I decided to stay in Yangon as I need to get souvenirs for my friends, family and colleagues. I already have about ten paper umbrellas and a couple lacquerware pieces from Bagan.

Adam had an interesting question for Than Tun today. Since he has moved to his house he was wondering how to dispose of his garbage. He says the pile is just getting higher and higher and he wondered if he should bury it or burn it. I suppose because I live at the hotel I never considered those issues. It was quite an entertaining conversation. Than Tun, ever the pragmatist, says he should ask his neighbour about the collection. I can see him secretly laughing at us. Apparently, every ward has an area where the garbage is disposed.

Several days ago, Mima told me that she wanted to give me a Myanmar traditional dress as a gift. She said she has a friend who makes the dresses whom she will invite to the office to take my measurements. True to her word, her friend appeared close to quitting time the next day and took my measurements. Today, three days later, Mima presents me with a traditional Myanmar dress. I thank her, give her a hug and go to the washroom to change into it. The top part is white and green and the bottom is green and black. Than Tun says he is honoured that I am wearing the traditional Myanmar dress and I get lots of thumbs up from the girls. They take loads of pictures. I love it very much and may wear it to church when I get back to Barbados. Later that night I have drinks and tapas with Johnathan, Finn and Lynette from Singapore who works for a children's charity. We share a few pitchers of sangria and eat tapas while we take selfies and talk about everything under the sun. Lynette is pleasant, delightful and good-natured and now Finn and Johnathan will have another friend when I leave. She tells us we should check out a shop called Pomelo for our souvenirs.

FOR THE LOVE OF COCONUT OIL

Thursday, August 21, 2014

I was complaining just the night before about how dry my hair was after I washed it on Monday and about the trials I have been having with finding hair products for my type of hair in Myanmar. Today when I arrive at the office there was a little gift bag on my desk with coconut oil.

When I read the label and peek into the bag, I see that my gift is from Finn and it is the Pure Fiji brand. I immediately run over to his desk to thank him. We have become so conditioned to expect bad things happening and people not being nice and genuine that when good things happen and people are nice it is a shock to our system.

Going home has been preoccupying my thoughts lately. I think about the comment Luke, a colleague in the Singapore office, made to me about hoping I can settle back in quickly to the team in the Eastern Caribbean. It bothers me a little. Was it meant to unsettle me about returning? Perhaps not, but I do hope I can settle back into my life in Barbados.

ASTON MARTINS, PORSCHES AND CHILD BEGGARS

Friday, August 22, 2014

The coconut oil from Finn worked miracles! I applied some to my hair yesterday evening and I was able to comb my hair through without any challenges and it felt amazing when I woke up this morning. I recall my mother using coconut oil in my hair as a child, but I hadn't used that stuff for years.

At the office this morning I am so heartened when Than Tun tells me that the team will miss me and that I have been so good to them. I tell him that they are the ones who have been good to me and I will miss them so much. They are really bright and the best team that I have worked with. The department is fairly quiet today. Than Tun and Htun Htun have left for their management development training, Win Tin is on sick leave and Mima is on casual leave as her grandmother is ill and she had to travel to the Pyay District to be with her.

I am having a reasonably good day until after I leave the French bakery. I am usually in high spirits after visiting the bakery as it is one of my favourite places in Yangon. However, this afternoon is different.

A child seller/beggar starts running behind me to encourage me to buy something. I feel the tapping of little hands on my bum in an effort to get my attention, but I do not look around. I know I will never forget this experience and how terrible I felt about the encounter. Here I am in my fancy shoes and clothes and nice jewellery compared to her shabby and needy appearance. It is hard for me to see someone in need and ignore them, especially when I have the means to assist. However, the expats were told by HR not to give money to child beggars. This was repeated to us by Lynette one night when we were chatting with her at The Lab. Lynette explained that these children should be in school and we are only keeping them in poverty by giving them money. Yet, my heart breaks.

Child beggars are often victims of human trafficking and the money they earn begging goes to organised criminals who are enslaving children. What happens when the child grows up? They are often pushed into prostitution. I feel really badly and this incident clearly affects the remainder of my afternoon. Than Tun from my department sees me and asks if I am okay and if I have a migraine. I just nod and smile. I am not sure how to explain the incident to him since he is from Myanmar himself. It makes me think about the Save the Children Charity and I get online and make a donation. I know it will not be enough and the money probably won't reach that particular child, but I hope it will reach some child in need. It doesn't help that I have been feeling a bit emotional about leaving and wondering if I am making the right choice.

The incident makes me want to bawl, but I have to keep it together because I am still in the office and have many more hours to go. Finn, Elliot and I had been chatting only yesterday about the disparity of wealth in Yangon. Elliot said he saw about three Aston Martins yesterday and we had just been commenting on the Porsche that was parked outside the French bakery. I will never understand how some people seem to have so much and others have so little. I am aware of poverty in Barbados, but it seems to be so glaring here in Myanmar. It was also only yesterday that I read that another company did an audit of their sites and found that some of the subcontractors had been using child labour. The child labour problem here is heartwrenching.

SOUVENIR SHOPPING

Saturday, August 23, 2014

I finally make it to lunch at around 1:30 p.m. which is an hour later than Finn and I had planned. Since the mobile launch at the beginning of August, we are no longer required to go into the office on Saturday, so the gang took the opportunity to have some fun last night. This is what happens when you have a night out at Union Bar and then 50th Street Bar for dirty martinis – you can't wake up and get your act together.

After lunch, Finn and I go to Pomelo just as Lynette suggested to buy some souvenirs for our respective trips home. It is a fair-trade marketplace supporting social businesses throughout Myanmar. Pomelo provides its artisan partners with training and education as well as economic rewards. Every purchase made contributes to social and economic change in some of Myanmar's most marginalised communities. The products offered for sale range from reclaimed teak candle holders made by former street children who have been trained in traditional carpentry to handmade soap made by refugee women in Kachin. At least we are doing our small part to help. I get some lovely notebooks covered in traditional printed fabric for my girl crew, cosmetic bags and longyis for family and a traditional onesie outfit for my baby cousin whom I have not met yet.

Later that night I go for pizza at The Pizza Company and Swensen's for ice cream with Elliot and Vlado. They treat me like I am their little sister. We later have a drink at Coffee Circles. We sit outside and it feels good to be out of the hotel and just doing stuff which is normal — like pizza and ice cream — and that we often take for granted in the Western world. I have a lively chat with Vlado and Elliot about books, which ranged from *Steppenwolf* to *The Trouser People* to *Father Frank*. On the way to find a taxi a little child worker tries to sell us flowers and Vlado has a talk with her. I can't hear what he is telling her since I am already a few yards ahead and had only turned around when I realised he had stopped. I want to walk back to where they are and pick her up and tuck her into bed. It is close to midnight and she should be in bed, not out on the streets working.

Sunday, August 24, 2014

Today is an uneventful day for me and I don't mind one bit. I sleep in late and return to Pomelo to purchase a dress for Skye (my friend Juann's daughter) and a couple more souvenirs. I had forgotten about Skye yesterday. I spend most of the evening resting and watching HBO and Fashion TV.

MIXED EMOTIONS

Monday, August 25, 2014

I end up oversleeping and so I miss breakfast. I just have enough time to get ready and make my way downstairs for my ride to work. As the time draws nearer, I have mixed emotions about leaving. Around lunch time I see Khin Papa and she asks, "Sa pi bi la?" and I tell her not yet.

"Sa pi bi la?" literally means "Have you finished your lunch?" I ask her the same thing, but she has already had lunch, so I ask her, "Bar hin nesar le?", translated to mean "What curry did you have for lunch?" She responds that she had chicken curry. I have lunch alone today. Elliot and Su had to go to Bago, Adam and Finn are in meetings and Khin Papa has already had her lunch.

Tuesday, August 26, 2014

Earlier tonight seven of us — Adam, Elliot, Vlado, Htet Htet, Su, Khin Papa and I — went bowling. I got the ball in the gutter more times than I was able to knock over the pins and they laughed and clapped for me each time I was victorious. Even the scorer girl cheered when I was finally able to knock over some pins. I am not going to be the next professional bowler, but I was having a ton of fun. As we were bowling and hanging out Khin Papa wanted to know why I have to go home. I explained to her that I have to go back to my substantive role in the Caribbean and I will miss her. Boy, are goodbyes hard! And I know that this is just the beginning.

Wednesday, August 27, 2014

One thing I can say about Yangon is it truly helped me to open my heart. It feels surreal that I am actually going home in a few days. It feels like the time flew very quickly. Than Tun asks if I will still have the same email address and how much it costs to fly to Barbados. I really hope to get him there one day. For my final night in Yangon, we have drinks at The Lab and everyone comes to say goodbye. There is such an outpouring of warmth and laughter that I ask myself: Why am I leaving again?

GIFTS AND GOODBYES

Thursday, August 28, 2014

Today is my final day in the Yangon office. Even though I don't cry I feel very sad about leaving. Mima and Nu Nu hold my bag and walk with me down the stairs to our final legal team dinner. I love them and I will miss them very much. The atmosphere is lively at the team dinner. We sit upstairs at Ginki Kids Restaurant in the partially open-air layout.

I must admit that it was not what I expected when I heard the name Ginki Kids. I thought it was maybe like a kid's fast-food spot like Chuck E. Cheese in the U.S., but it turned out to be a lovely venue. The restaurant is located in a small relatively nondescript two-storey red-bricked wall building in the residential Golden Valley area in Yangon. Pictures of Kurt Cobain, Elvis Presley, the Beatles and Bob Marley are on the walls. The restaurant serves both Eastern and Western dishes. We choose from the Eastern dishes which include Thai, Chinese and Myanmar dishes since this is probably the last time I will get to experience them. After we finish eating and drinking, the team presents me with a gift. It is an antique traditional lacquerware jewellery box, black with a brass turtle on the cover. I vaguely remember telling Mima that turtles were my favourite animals and talking about the nesting turtles in Barbados. When I open the box, there is a set with traditional Myanmar pearls, a necklace and a bracelet in it. I love it. I know I will treasure them as long as I live.

Friday, August 29, 2014

It is my last day in Yangon. I wake up at my usual time and feel strange that I am not going into the office since it is Friday and a work day. I sit quietly on the bed and think to myself that this is the final time I will be waking up in this hotel. I get up slowly and go to the shower, cognisant that this will also be my last time in that shower. When I get out, I turn the TV to Al Jazeera one last time. As I get dressed, I remember Luke's words about settling back in the Caribbean. I think about Mima and the others and what they may be doing at this time and what the department will be like without me. When I am ready, I give the place a once-over to make sure I haven't left anything and I look out the window one last time at the monastery. Thankfully, Finn and I are departing at the same time and so our driver Chok collects Finn first from his apartment and then me from the hotel and takes us to the airport. It is nice that I will have Finn's company on these long flights — first, three hours to Malaysia and then 13 hours to Heathrow. I will get to savour the last remaining hours of our friendship, even though this does not lessen the sadness. In Malaysia, we purchase day passes for the VIP lounge. The lounge is a classy, relaxing space and I am thankful that it is not packed. There's a bar that serves alcohol so we both order a cold glass of white wine. There are plenty of windows with views of the planes and loads of seating with charging points and some USB sockets, free newspapers and free magazines. I pick up a copy of *Tatler Malaysia*.

There is no shortage of food and a wide array of selections in the lounge. There is a really nice noodle café serving curry, various noodles and chicken dumplings. There is also another food area where chefs prepare grilled sandwiches like cheese and veggies on paninis, tuna sandwiches and various wraps. The buffet offers pasta, potatoes, dim sum, veggie dishes, soft and hot drinks. I order a chicken wrap and get some dim sum from the buffet. We drink some more wine and relax until our flight number is announced.

It is a pity I will have to do the last eight-hour leg without him.

GETTING HOME

Saturday, August 30, 2014

I make it to Heathrow and say goodbye to Finn. We hug for a long time. I will miss him and Johnathan. We promise to stay in touch. He walks off to get his flight to Ireland and I take a taxi from Heathrow to Gatwick which costs £152. It is slightly cheaper if you book in advance, but somehow, with all the packing and saying goodbye to everyone, I had forgotten to do it before I left Yangon.

* * *

At 2 p.m. I touch down in Barbados and I smile. I am home again. My Auntie Ann is waiting for me when I get to the Arrivals Hall. She runs over to me as soon as I step through the automatic doors and embraces me in the tightest of hugs as though to close the time apart. She tells me, without letting go, that she is happy I made it back safely. She is hugging me and swaying from side to side and, to avoid becoming emotional and so she would loosen her grip, I laugh and remind her I haven't showered since I left Yangon on Friday. She eventually releases me. She goes to pay the parking and then we walk to where my car is parked and I get in my car and drive home like I had never left. It feels good to drive myself after three months. I finally satisfy my three-month craving for KFC and I slowly savour it. I am home. Dido's "Thank You" is playing on the radio. I fondly remember that this song used to play every time Mima's phone rang. Thank you, Yangon, for giving me the best days of my life. You challenged me and humbled me. I know I am not the same, but being away from what is familiar does that.

LESSONS I LEARNT SO FAR ON THIS JOURNEY CALLED LIFE

1. Don't be afraid to try new things; they may surprise you.

2. True happiness will never come from material things; it comes from within; it comes from giving to others and it comes from surrounding yourself with incredible people.

3. God places the people we need in our lives. Good, bad or indifferent, they are there to teach us. Learn each lesson well.

4. You have to be with yourself 24/7, 365 days a year (366 in a leap year), so learn to love the you that you are, and the you that you are striving to be.

5. Sometimes the best thing you can do is let go of a situation. Accept that it was not meant to be. When you let go, you free yourself up for something better.

6. Life happens. Don't take everything so seriously. Laugh at yourself.

7. And most of all, you don't have to end up where you started. You can be born into a particular circumstance with limited resources, but you don't have to let that define you. You are ultimately in control of your life so you can change your story to what you want it to be.